More DANGEROUS

THAN

TERRORISTS

How to Stop Economic Espionage that Threatens Our Way of Life!

By BJ Williamson

Lanite Publishing, LLC

Dedications

This book is dedicated to the great American leaders who had the foresight to invest in technology, inventors who improved our quality of life, and to those who bravely fought and paid the great price for our freedom.

God Bless America.

Contents

Introduction

After seeing mass layoffs of Americans by American corporations, I began searching for answers. My search led me to discover that this was about much more than job losses. I uncovered some disturbing foreign agendas. More Dangerous than Terrorists reveals how our way of life and national security are in jeopardy. This book is a culmination of several years of research.

Note: Because of the extensive number of sources reference numbers are provided in [brackets] arranged numerically in a list at the back of the book. Certain words have *italics* and <u>underlining</u> added for emphasis in quotations and/or key points. Because it would be burdensome to readers to repeatedly state: "according to" named source, under document heading, by these authors, on this date" each time a source is mentioned you should read with the understanding that information cited is according to the source.

Chapter 1

More Dangerous Than

Terrorists

Outsourcing is a Trojan Horse

There is a vital link between our economy and our national security. The more money and high tech jobs US citizens have, the more money and power the US government has. For every US job lost to a foreign worker the US government tax base erodes and money that would have gone to the US government instead flows to a foreign government.

Enemies know that our military is dependent on our economy, and that harming the US economy strikes at the life line of our military. [419]

What good does it do if we have the most advanced military in the world if our economy crashes, and we do not have the money to supply our troops and buy fuel?

The focus on terrorists and the war in Iraq diverted our attention while some foreign nations were accelerating the outsourcing attacks on our economy and national security. What a Pyrrhic victory it would be if we win the war on terror, and lose the larger war on our economy.

Pentagon Warns of New WMD Threat

In October 2012, a Pentagon report identified new *weapons of mass destruction* (WMD) threats to our nation. Given our formidable military strength, a military confrontation was thought to be unlikely. Instead it warned enemies may use a new WMD strategy of *"cyber, electronic and financial attacks."* [122]

The Pentagon report referred to a Chinese military book, Unrestricted Warfare, written in 1999 that advocated attacks using currency manipulation, planting computer viruses, and causing stock market crashes. The report said China has 180,000 cyber spies that steal our technology and compromise our security. It speculated that the May 6, 2010, stock *"flash crash"* a drop of 10%, may have been an covert "economic attack" done by terrorists or a foreign country. Attackers may have tampered with computer algorithms to allow massive anonymous short sells, or it could have been done by a nation holding major US debt. [122]

Warning "Pearl Harbor" Cyber Attack Threat

Leon Panetta in his June 2011 Senate confirmation hearing warned of, *"a strong likelihood that the next Pearl Harbor"* could be a cyber attack that cripples our infrastructure, business, and government computer systems. [952]

One month after Panetta's warning, a *Fox News* report, "Pentagon Discloses Largest-Ever Cyber Theft," reported that a few months earlier our *Pentagon suffered the worst cyber attack by a foreign country in our nation's history.* An astounding *"24,000 files containing Pentagon data were stolen from a defense industry computer network in a single intrusion."* [954] Why was this data on the Internet!?

In this book we will explore how foreign nations were able to leapfrog and gain knowledge, access and technology to pose new WMD threats against our country.

CIA Warned About Outsourcing Risks in 2001

At a cyber security hearing back in June 2001, Lawrence K. Gershwin, a top CIA science and technology intelligence officer, cautioned about the dangers of outsourcing: *"While we may be working with American companies on issues at some point, there are contracts and subcontracts, ...It gets hard to tell who's doing the work for you."* [434]

Gershwin warned our security was too focused on terrorists. [435] He said: *"more than terrorists, foreign governments are projected to be the main threat to US computers over the next 5 to 10 years."* [206]

Our government security was so focused swatting at the terrorist bee buzzing in their car, they did not see the speeding outsourcing train barreling down full speed towards their side door.

HINDUSTANTIMES.COM REPORT INDIA IW THREAT

Days after Gershwin's testimony, the *HindustanTimes.com* wrote that while he named Russia and China as Information Warfare (IW) threats, *The Washington Times* reported that US military officials said *India was also an IW threat.* [206]

Tellingly, this *HindustanTimes* article cited espionage statistics about foreign attacks on our computers. It reported that when we connect a computer to the Internet we can expect to be hacked in just eight hours. (So if you have a patent idea or a valuable business idea, don't put it on a computer that will be connected to the internet.) It also reported that if *a US university connects an unsecured computer to the internet it can expect to be hacked by foreign spies in only 45 minutes!*

What did foreign nations want? The *HindustanTimes* article elaborated that the CIA was concerned foreign *"adversaries"* engaged in espionage and sabotage of US computer networks were "transferring" (i.e. stealing) US technology and *threatening the US's ability to compete economically.* [206]

CIA Radical Change in 2005

During his 2004 campaign Bush reassured India that outsourcing would continue if he won. (See <u>Democracy Hijacked</u> book). Following his re-election, there was a radical change in our CIA.

After the election a 2005 CIA report, "Mapping the Global Future," *disturbingly glossed over the "transfer" of strategic US technology. It said that <u>multinational corporations were the "**key agents of change in dispersing technology.**"</u>* [445] The report shockingly wrote: *"whether the technologies are acquired through a country's own basic research or from technology leaders" i.e. the US*, the key was applying *"globally available technologies."* [445] When did US technology become *"globally available"*?

This CIA report inspired *The Times of India* to write, "2020 AD: India may Outshine US," – the opening line read, *"The rise of China and India as global players is <u>heralding an Asian Century in place of a receding American Century, a US intelligence report said</u> on Thursday."* [405]

Our CIA lamented that after the September 11th attacks it was more difficult to attract foreign students. The report claimed we needed foreign students because <u>the number of American engineering graduates had fallen 20%</u>. The important bit of information omitted by the report was that the number of Americans pursuing engineering degrees declined because of decreased job opportunities. The H-1B visas let foreign student graduates take entry level engineering jobs that should have gone to Americans.

Conversely, Bruce Berkowitz's 1995 book, <u>War in the Information Age</u>, warned that foreign students could be used by foreign nations: *"<u>A more subtle alternative might be to send several hundred promising students to school to become computer experts and covert hackers.</u>"* [420] Despite this and other warnings, we are admitting hundreds of thousands of foreign students yearly!

National Intelligence Council (NIC) analysts who wrote the report gathered *predictions from over 1,000 consultants by attending 30 conferences around the world in 2004*. [405] (Imagine if the CIA had sent analysts to consult with the Nazis prior to WWII when Hitler was preparing to conquer the world. It is not hard to guess what nations they would have forecasted to rise and fall in power.) Analysts wrote, *"the benefits of globalization won't be global."* It even said that anti-Americanism is expected to decrease as the *"face of globalization"* becomes less Western and more Asian. [445]

This CIA report surmised: *"how China and India exercise their growing power and whether they relate cooperatively or competitively to other powers in the international system are key uncertainties."* [445] It is apparent to most Americans that China and India are competing against us. India's Prime Minister in 2005 proclaimed that India and China *"could together reshape the world order."* [271] China and India signed multibillion dollar bilateral trade agreements. [271] They pursue nationalist goals while promoting 'globalization' to the US.

China's competitive intentions are evident. For example:

■ *China referred to its first CPU as the "Intel slayer." The Chinese government financed the company run by CEO Zeng Ming. Guess where Ming was previously employed–Intel as a circuit design engineer for 10 years. Did Intel executives realize they were training their Chinese competition when Ming took an American's job? Ming returned to China in 2003. [522] Did Ming get an H-1B visa in 1993?*

India also plotted to compete against us. For example:

■ *The siliconindia magazine held a two day California Conference: "Plotting Tech Battles for the 21st Century" in 1999. The "battle" targets identified were our semiconductor industry, telecom industry, and software industry. The keynote: "India on the Horizon." Topics included: "India: Land of Opportunities Again" on how IT could benefit India's economy, and "India's destiny in the technology world." [313]*

"Transformed World" Report!

In 2008, another report by the National Intelligence Council, "Global Trends 2025: a Transformed World," again *predicted the decline of our nation*, because of the ***"historic transfer of relative wealth and economic power from West to East."*** The CIA should be advising us on how to protect our intellectual property not fawning over a *"historic transfer"* of our technology and money to Asia. [950]

Our CIA was telling us to submit to the "transfer" of our economic and military power to China and India. They wanted us to lie down and rollover. However, our nation's symbol is the eagle, and eagles do not rollover when attacked, they soar higher. Once the political correctness blindfold is removed, Americans will see clearly once again. Our nation will soar free from the fetters of outsourcing.

Warnings Not Heeded H-1B National Security Risk

For over two decades intelligence experts repeatedly warned our leaders that they were putting our economy and national security at risk by hiring foreign H-1B programmers. They warned that foreign programmers may: *plant viruses, spy, steal technology, skim money from financial transactions, alter voting results, and more.* [90]

Dr. Gene A. Nelson in 1999 testified to Congress: *"There is a substantial security risk associated with the H-1B program. Department of Defense contractors are selecting foreign nationals for R&D work because they offer a short-term cost advantage."* [224] Nelson claimed the number of foreign workers was overwhelming US counterintelligence. And, he said the FBI knew Asian organized crime networks in the US helped members of their ethnic group get H-1B visas, and then pressured them to steal. [224]

The 3 year "temporary" H-1B visa program jeopardizing our national security is 23 years old!

Many Surprises Ahead

Leaders in our businesses, our government and even our universities appear to have violated the public trust and jeopardized our economy and national security. We will explore the Information Warfare (IW) threat. Then we will proceed to peel back layer upon layer of espionage and economic attacks by foreign nations that have been kept hidden from you. Researching our foreign debt uncovers many surprising twists and turns and deceptions.

Chapter 2

Destructive Foreign Trade

Deficit

The United States was a creditor nation -- the richest nation on Earth.

Because of "Globalization" the US is now the largest debtor nation on Earth.

Adm. Mike Mullen warned that our nation's debt was the biggest threat to our national security. He said, *"I was shown the figures the other day by the comptroller of the Pentagon that said that the <u>interest on our debt is $571 billion in 2012</u>. That is noticeably, about the size of the defense budget. It is not sustainable."* [951]

The highest paid executives and politicians in our nation's history are ruining our nation. It's like being in a relay race, where our team's first three runners left the competition in the dust. We were miles ahead of the competition when the baton was passed, all the next runner had to do was run at an average pace, and the competition could not possibly catch up.

But no, our runner passed our baton to the competition. Generations of Americans had our nation so advanced technically and economically that other countries could not catch up. Then our leaders passed our technology and jobs to foreign nations. They threw the race for personal gain. Offshoring is destroying our country economically.

Competing Against Us with Our Designs!

The media represents that our trade deficit results from Americans buying "foreign" goods and services. However, *the US trade deficit was not created by US citizens' insatiable demand for Chinese, Indian and Mexican goods and services.* Rather, our trade deficit results from buying the same products and services that were originally invented and produced in America by Americans.

What the media doesn't tell you is that executives used money in our corporations to build facilities in foreign countries. And then, they "transferred" our jobs and technology to these foreign nations. As a direct result, China and India and other foreign countries are selling "American" goods and services back to America. We were importing everything from cars, to clothes, to televisions, to furniture, to jewelry, to toys and more.

Compounding the offense, US products and services produced in these foreign subsidiaries were also being sold around the world! This harmed our country globally because it took away foreign market opportunities for products and services produced in America.

In 2000 we began running trade deficits in advanced technologies with countries in Asia, with Mexico, and with Ireland. <u>None of these countries were the inventors of this advanced technology</u>. [81] Our government failed to stop this raiding of our technology. "Our Nation's Surprising Technology Trade Deficit," a 2008 report said that, "*<u>our nation's hi-tech deficit reached new record highs</u>.*" From 2002-2007 *our high tech trade deficit with China grew 473%, and Mexico was even worse growing by 492%.* The US trade deficit for electronics products reached $16.5 billion. And for information and communications technology products our trade deficit ran $57.5 billion! [671]

Had our corporate coffers not been raided we would have no trade deficit with China, Mexico and many other countries.

From Creditor Nation to Debtor Nation

Our Net International Investment Position (NIIP) plunged drastically, "*the United States went from the world's strongest international asset position to the world's largest liability position.*" [570]

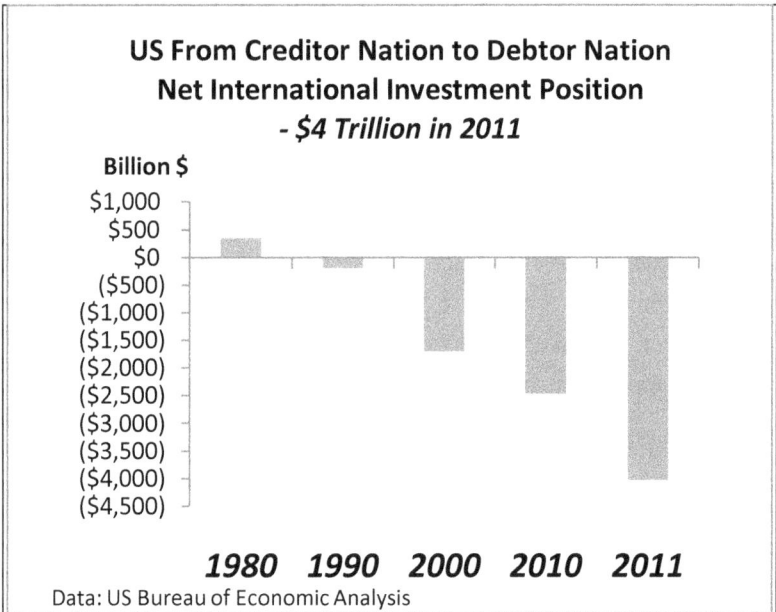

Data: US Bureau of Economic Analysis

From 1980 to 2000, we went from being a $350 billion creditor nation, to a $1.7 trillion debtor nation. [488]

The biggest part of our foreign debt was US government debt obligations held by foreigners. [570]

In 2007 we still had the world's biggest GNP at $13.3 trillion. However, we also had the world's biggest national debt of $8.6 trillion, worst foreign debt at $2.1 trillion, and unemployment higher than 38 countries. [537] [179] [490] [583]

Our NIIP hit minus $4 trillion in 2011! Our GNP ran $15.5 trillion. "IMF bombshell: Age of America Nears End," by *marketwatch.com* reported the IMF *forecasted that in 2016 China's economy will surpass ours.* This is a shocking given that in 2001 our economy was three times the size of China's. [928]

No Trade is Better than Bad Trade

Some trade relations have been losing propositions for us. Much of our record level deficits did not result from trade, but rather from a dispossession of our wealth and future income. [167]

Our media encourages US citizens to spend to stimulate our economy. Yet, buying foreign made goods does not stimulate our economy. It increases our trade deficit and causes job losses, which in turn harms our economy.

Consumers buying goods and services produced by US citizens stimulate our economy. This puts money into the hands of Americans who are also US consumers. Without jobs Americans cannot purchase goods and services.

In contrast, buying foreign made goods and services creates crippling debt–unless of course, foreign countries buy enough products and services made by Americans to balance the trade.

Trade implies a reciprocal exchange. Offshore outsourcing does not involve trade. It is a one-way export of American jobs. Because goods and services produced by the offshored jobs are imported to our country, this is a double blow to our economy.

Analyzing the lopsided trade deficit, The Economic Policy Institute estimated that from 1993 through 2000, our country experienced a net loss of 3 million jobs. [141] Another 3 million manufacturing jobs were lost from 2001 to 2006 because our government promoted "free trade." It was "free" to foreign nations but painfully costly to Americans. [511]

Even more disturbing, in attempts to reduce the foreign debt, our leaders sold high tech "dual use" (commercial/military) technology products to foreign countries.

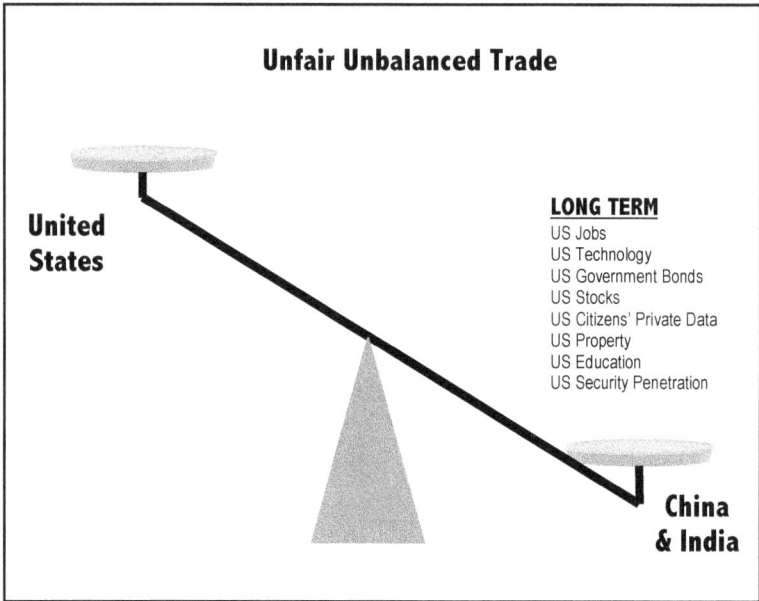

Paying the Same Wages Does Not Make Theft OK

Some US politicians naively think that the solution for competitiveness is to require foreign workers be paid higher wages. We need politicians smart enough to realize this is folly. If our technology is distributed globally, and if all workers are paid at the same level of wages; then both China and India would collect tax revenues 5 times those collected by the US government.

Paying the workers the same does not make theft all right. Imagine if a new soft drink company managed to get some spies planted who stole the formula from a well known company. Is everything ok provided the startup pays its employees the same wages as the company it stole the formula from? –Of course not.

Greenspan's Role In Decline of America

No wonder our nation has an economic crisis. It appears the Federal Reserve is undermining our nation by pushing a globalist agenda. A 2009 *computerworld.com* article, "Greenspan: H-1B Cap Would Make U.S. Workers 'Privileged Elite'," reported that Alan Greenspan, (Federal Reserve Chairman 1987–2006) testified to a U.S. Senate subcommittee the H-1B visa quota cap was too small.

He said increasing H-1B quotas could help solve our housing crisis. [929] This is outrageous. Because of H-1Bs and offshoring millions of Americans lost their jobs and were forced to default on their mortgages. So Greenspan wants to bring in more H-1Bs so that they can buy vacant American homes.

Greenspan blamed Americans' education for our job losses. He pointed to the high number of foreign graduate students to justify his stance. [929] So he thinks a 27-30 year old foreign graduate student with 6-8 years of college competing against a 22 year old American college graduate with 4 years of college shows superiority. It would better be explained as a cruel abuse of young Americans who are being denied job opportunities created by their parents and grandparents. His claim of superiority of foreign workers is debunked in the book False Prophets of False Profits.

Despite our high unemployment, in 2011 Greenspan was again trying to remove H-1B quota caps. He claimed young Americans were being paid less than their baby boomer parents because they were not as productive. [930] It is more like because H-1B visas depressed their wages.

Greenspan's arguing that Americans should not have more advanced jobs is the same as arguing that our nation should not have a more advanced economy and military. Is he advocating the downfall of our nation? He is faulting us for investing and inventing and being successful.

It is Time to End our Destructive Trade Deficits

We need a government that will protect our jobs and intellectual property so that our nation can compete globally. Congress needs to revoke H-1B visas, offshoring tax incentives and stop funding offshore business development.

Most importantly, our government needs to create a pro business environment here in the US. There should be tax breaks and incentives for companies that are owned and run by US citizens, and employ US citizens. The paperwork load needs to be reduced and simplified so that US companies can focus on generating jobs, products, and profits.

There are many things we can do. For example, one alternative to offshoring proposed in *Machine Design* was for large US corporations to contract unprofitable operations to small agile US companies. Small American companies would have several advantages over offshoring such as lower shipping costs and faster turnaround. Being smaller they would be more efficient and have less overhead with fewer layers of expensive bureaucracy to support. Moreover, US companies that offshore rarely get the promised cost savings. In contrast, the article said US companies contracting with small American suppliers were more likely to actually get the 45% cost savings. *And, even more important, large US companies using this strategy do not have to do a "knowledge transfer" to a foreign nation creating potential foreign competitors.* [398]

Another alternative to offshoring is to automate production processes more. This is something Americans have excelled at doing from inventing harvesting machines, to computers, to robots and more. While jobs would be lost to automation, at least we would not be incurring more foreign debt.

Chapter 3

Our American Birthright

Then: Taxpayer funded research created American jobs and made America the world's technology leader.

Now: Taxpayer funded research jobs are misdirected to foreign workers and jeopardize our technology leadership.

Executives lied to Congress to get H-1B and other foreign worker legislation passed. After the false claims of worker shortages, cost savings, and that foreign workers were the best and brightest were debunked, executives attempted to justify their actions by saying Americans had no claim to our high tech jobs. For example, former HP executive Carly Fiorina said: "*There is no job that is America's God-given right anymore. We have to compete for jobs.*" [114] [222] Executives used this argument to attempt to defend channeling our jobs, technology, and money to foreign countries.

However, Americans worked for generations to create our technologies. We invested billions in US corporations and tax funded research with the understanding that the research would benefit Americans. We financed education, research, and vital infrastructure that enabled American corporations to flourish. [546]

The US did not become the world's leader in technology though happenstance. US invented and/or taxpayer-funded technology belongs to Americans and is our birthright and a birthright to our children.

Our Tax Dollars Generated New Technology

Following our technology achievements during World War II, our government invested in research *to strengthen our national security, and to advance our country socially and economically*. [185]

Our taxes paid most of the bill for high risk *"basic research.."* This involves creating something new that did not exist before such as creating the first computer and the first software program. Imagine conceptualizing a computer when no computer existed.

Basic research is like prospecting for gold. Most of what is scoured through has little value and is discarded. After spending billions of dollars and years of research, most projects do not pan out into profitable inventions. However, if you look long and hard enough you may find that rare nugget of gold.

Because basic research can take many years, is high risk and very expensive, executives lobby our Congress for us to "seed" i.e. fund basic research. [170] Industry R&D does some basic research; however, it often prefers to take tax funded technology breakthroughs that it fine tunes and packages to sell for profit. [484]

Our taxes funded R&D that generated almost half of the US economic growth from the early 1950's to 2001. [170]

Where did our research money go? US government research laboratories get about 25% of our tax funded research money. Our tax dollars also fund research done by nonprofit organizations such as Federally Funded Research and Development Centers (FFRDCs). And our universities also get a large amount of R&D funding from government grants.

However, "*the largest share of federally funded R&D is performed by industrial firms under contracts*." [170]

Did NSF Violate its Mission?

The National Science Foundation (NSF) was established in 1950, by our government to support education and *"basic research." The mission of the NSF is: "to ensure that the **United States** maintains leadership in scientific discovery and the development of new technologies."* [548]

However, in *1999, Dr. Gene Nelson testified before the US House of Representatives that* he traced claims that we had a high tech worker shortage *to our NSF. He found we had a surplus, not a shortage, of high tech American workers when the H-1B visa was passed in 1990.* He believed the NSF made the claims to increase its budget. *This H-1B legislation jeopardized our technology leadership when it was misused to displace millions of Americans with foreign workers.* [47]

"TECHNOLOGY WITHOUT BORDERS CONFERENCE"

Rajat Gupta co-chaired the *"Technology Without Borders Global iit2005 Conference."* Atma Sahu head of the *Conference Publications Team* was a US professor *"engaged in consulting with the National Science Foundation (NSF), the Department of Education, the Department of Defense..."* He *acknowledged international research collaborations by US faculty pose conflict of interest and financial risks, and jeopardize intellectual property.* Yet, he *"serves as National President IIT-Roorkee in North America." Sahu called our NSF and Department of Science and Technology (DST) "**international research agencies"!*** [523]

In 2001, Sahu held a *"NSF-DST...research collaboration workshop"* at IIT-Roorkee in India! [523] Did our taxes pay for a collaboration that jeopardizes our technology leadership?

Kesh Narayanan, NSF Director of Industrial Innovation in charge of allocating a $100 million US research budget, was listed as an attendee. [485] Speakers encouraged Indian Institute of Technology (IIT) alumni to *obtain subcontracting from the US government.* [523]

Companies Got the Most Tax Funded R&D Money

While businesses claim to spend a lot on research, when you dig a little deeper, you discover that much of what appears to be industry research spending traces back to government contracts funded by our tax dollars.

The biggest share of our tax funded research money goes to companies via federal contracts. Congress doles out our research money via authorizations and appropriations. It is a fragmented and flawed process entangled in politics and power. [170]

Our tax dollars are channeled to hundreds of programs funding business research that were supposed to create jobs for Americans. However a 1995 investigation uncovered that *the opposite was happening*.

Small companies that generated nearly two-thirds of new jobs got less than 4% of the money. [172] While from 1990 to 1995, *GE, IBM, AT&T, Amoco, GM, DuPont and Citicorp* collected $293 million at the same time they cut 329,000 US citizens' jobs. And, semiconductor companies received over $1 billion, yet *almost half the jobs were offshored to foreign workers in Ireland, Malaysia, Singapore, Taiwan and South Korea!* Many Fortune 500 companies received millions while employing visa workers and offshoring our jobs. [172]

But, that's not all. Companies also profited from 'partnering' with our government R&D labs, and our university tax funded R&D programs. Politicians argue that these programs are not corporate welfare because the companies split the costs. However, our government did little to track or audit how much companies actually paid. [172]

Critics of these research programs labeled them corporate welfare, because both US political parties became involved in pork barrel politics. [170]

COMPANIES PROFITED FROM US GOVERNMENT LABS

In the early 1980's, our government decided to use its huge network of 700 government labs and 30,000 scientists and engineers to *help the US economically compete with foreign nations*. [172]

Our federal research labs already had a great deal of technology that could be transferred into commercial products. *The justification for opening our government labs to businesses: "Why shouldn't American industry reap the benefits of the expertise that existed in the labs? asked spinoff advocates. After all,* **taxpayers were paying billions for it***."* [172]

The payback to taxpayers was supposed to be enormous *yielding hundreds of thousands of high paying high tech jobs for Americans.*

However, *the results were dismal. It failed to produce the jobs and economic benefits promised.* A 1995, report, "How Billions in Taxes Failed to Create Jobs," found that many companies profiting from access to our government labs actually cut American jobs. Many companies that got the money laid off US citizens and set up offshore facilities. *The lack of adequate governmental oversight and controls yielded more "technology transfer" benefits to foreign nations competing against the US than to the US economy.* [172]

Much of the R&D funding we pay for is hidden from us. For example, the Department of Energy owns 30 labs. It partners with private companies and *underwrites their R&D costs*. It keeps *secret the details of agreements and the amount of taxpayer money it gives away to these partners.* [172] Executives from companies receiving money were in advisory groups that picked *"critical technologies"* to receive the money. *This puts the government in a position of influencing which energy companies will be most successful.* [172] Since we are paying for this energy research, we have a right to know what companies are getting this money and if they employ Americans or foreign workers.

COMPANIES PROFITED FROM UNIVERSITY TAX FUNDED PATENTS

To encourage businesses to partner with universities, the Bayh-Dole Act gave *"universities and small businesses the rights to own federally funded intellectual property and <u>grant exclusive licenses to companies.</u>"* [181] *Before Congress passed the Bayh-Dole Act in 1980, federal funding accounted for <u>67.1% of university research</u> while industry provided only 6.9% of the funding.* [185] This Act was a good idea because only about 5% of university patents generated by taxes were marketed.

By 1999, the NSF was deeply involved in sponsoring partnership programs between our government, universities, and businesses. [185] Royalties from licensing patent rights became a lucrative source of money for US universities. The US patent office granted 34,542 patents to universities from 1994 through April of 2006. By 2004, over 200 universities were involved in "technology transfer." There were universities that *sold 100 or more license agreements a year.* [181] [182]

Federal grants fund nearly 60% of our university research. [170] Although our federal government had the authority to direct the licensing, it took a hands-off approach.

Some executives got greedy. Consumer outrage flared in 2004 when life saving drugs created using our taxes had markups as high as 400%. Protestors wanted our government to oversee the licensing process to lower prices. However, executives threatened that if our government controlled the licensing, they would stop marketing new technology created in our universities. [181]

In certain cases, companies that only paid a small portion of lab research *demanded rights to all of a university's research.* US universities objected. In turn, executives diverted R&D money to universities in China, India, Russia, and more. For example, in 2006 *an HP executive estimated that approximately half of HP's funding for university research went to universities in foreign countries.* [545]

US Military Agencies Created the Internet

The Internet was created by US government military agencies in 1969 to *streamline the exchange of military and scientific data stored on government computers in different locations.* [249] [295]

Our leaders foolishly deployed the Internet to foreign nations despite knowledge that it would be almost impossible to secure, and that it was dangerous because of its military applications. For example, in 2002, *the CIA discovered that both China and Russia were training soldiers on how to use the Internet to launch attacks.* [211]

"Kofi Annan's IT Challenge to Silicon Valley," a 2002 *CNet* article, called for the US to *"bridge the digital divide"* by giving away our technology to developing nations. [769]

The UN pressured us to give up control of the Internet. [429] Giving up control of the Internet would endanger our nation.

The Importance of Protecting Intellectual Property

When technology rights are protected and rewarded, inventiveness flourishes. US businesses, US government research, and US university labs flourished under the protections of US intellectual property laws and business laws.

Conversely, when technology is stolen it weakens motivation to do research and stifles creativity. Countries where property rights are not honored end up being poor countries.

R&D for the design of just one advanced microprocessor may cost a US company hundreds of millions of dollars. Because of the time and costs associated with inventions, our laws provide 17 years of patent protection. On the other hand, once invented, a new chip design can be stolen in an instant during a cyber attack.

Our American Birthright

Our investments in research made our country an economic and military powerhouse. We invented new technologies including the computer, the software industry, the telecom industry, the semiconductor, and much more. These technological advances improved our way of life, energized our economy, and provided superior military protections. When *"we the people"* invest our taxes to seed research and to create jobs, we have a right to declare the technology and jobs belong to Americans. [114] [222]

If you become CEO of a US corporation, you have no *"God-given right"* to personally profit by 'transferring' US intellectual property to foreign nations. It is like being picked for quarterback on Team America. As quarterback you don't have the right to accept money from the other team and throw them our ball. Nor does the referee (politician) have the right to accept bribes and throw the game offshore. Executives in companies that received millions in R&D benefits from federal contracts, our government labs, and our universities did not have the right to *'transfer' technology we paid for to foreign countries.* They were paid to ensure our technology leadership.

We did not invest our taxes to create technology and jobs to send overseas. We are funding our own economic demise and our own military threats.

What is more, *universities collecting royalties for licensing tax funded patents should have lowered college costs for young Americans.* Instead, college costs continued to soar. Did this money go to fund foreign students, or into the pockets of faculty or both?

Chapter 4

Executives "Wary of Being

Named"

If they weren't doing anything wrong there would be no need to hide.

When researching outsourcing and offshoring, article after article exposed that executives wanted to hide what they were doing. They wanted to keep US investors, US customers, and US politicians in the dark. Why? *"They are keeping quiet for fear of a backlash."* [100]

US executives required foreign outsourcing companies to sign nondisclosure agreements as a condition of obtaining offshore contracts. These executives *"guard information about their outsourcing activities as if they were state secrets."* [6]

If these executives were not doing anything wrong they would not be putting so much effort into hiding their offshoring activities. There was not a good way to spin this to convince US citizens what they were doing was justified.

Becoming the head of a US company does not give executives the right to exploit employees and investors for their own personal gain. Yet many foolishly compromised intellectual property secrets and laid off loyal American workers.

They have the Midas touch for creating fool's gold.

Executives Cover-up Job "Transfers"

Executives diverted billions of dollars earned from American operations, and billions invested in the United States stock market, to build facilities in high risk foreign countries. They spawned our foreign competition. These were big name US corporations including Microsoft, IBM, Goldman Sachs, Lehman Brothers, AT&T Wireless, and more. [100]

Executives did not want you to know what they were doing. For example, a 2002 InfoWorld article, "BPO Bound for Bombay" wrote that US executives *"outsourcing to India BPO firms are still wary of being named."* [76]

Another 2003 article, "The Offshore Value Chain," reported that hundreds of US companies had *invested heavily* to set up offshore subsidiaries; and, they *kept this "mostly invisible to casual observers at home."* This included companies like EDS and Accenture selling services and consulting. And it included high tech companies such Boeing and GE. [75]

During the 2004 US presidential election an article, "Silence is Golden for Outsourcing" by Anupama Chandrasekaran had the subheading: *"Mum's the word for U.S. companies exporting jobs to India and other countries."* The article said: *"The media, investors and analysts are often kept in the dark."* [89]

The secrecy continued. US corporations' offshoring outsourced work to Wipro in India did not want to be named according to a 2005 *U.S. News & World Report* article, "Bangalore's Big Dreams." Nonetheless, one list of Wipro's clients named: *"Morgan Stanley, Sun Microsystems, General Motors, Honeywell, Cisco, and Lucent."* Wipro's headcount grew by 300% from 2002 to early 2005, bringing the headcount of this one outsourcing company alone to nearly 42,000. [122]

Foreign Workers Trained to Lie to Americans

An ABC online news report in 2002 wrote: *"They may call themselves Lisa, or Val, but their real name could be Krishnamoorthi or Brajesh,... Big American corporations are increasingly turning their customer service calls and other back office business activities over to foreigners to save money. ...Agents at Talwar's center <u>do not disclose where they are</u>. "These people, they don't know we're in India," said one agent. "They just know that we are in Tempe, Arizona."* [130]

"<u>Companies that outsource to India would prefer to keep that under wraps</u>," reported a 2003 article, "Outsourcing to India." US Executives *required outsourcing firms to sign contracts promising not to divulge that they were a client.* Customer support workers in India were *"told to pick an American name such as John or Rose, instead of their real names like Jeetendra or Radha."* [90]

Why all the lying and deception? A 2005 survey found that 24% of Americans would stop doing business with a company if it offshored service support. The main issue was not quality of service; it was loyalty to the US. Americans said they would cut off business regardless of the quality of service. [80]

Executives often hid the number of jobs offshored to foreign workers by hiring an American outsourcing company such as IBM. This created an illusion that the outsourced work would be done in the US by US citizens. However, IBM employed many H-1Bs in the Unites States, and had offshore offices in India. [89]

In November 2006, IBM announced that its Research Lab in India had developed a technology to *help workers in India sound more American.* IBM planned to invest *$6 billion* more in India to build facilities and hire more workers. *IBM had already bought a call center company in 2004, which basically meant that IBM acquired 25,000 BPO workers in India.* [591]

Executives Supplied Foreign Espionage

Prior to "globalization," US executives tightly guarded proprietary company information. They restricted access to the manufacturing floor, prohibited cameras, and designated off limit areas. Security made it difficult for foreign spies to get access to even snap a few pictures of one design. These obstacles created formidable barriers to foreign espionage.

The following table exposes how obstacles were not only removed, but that executives supplied foreign competition with training, facilities, money, technology secrets, and more.

Executives Enabled Espionage	
Aided and Abetted Foreign Competition	
Historical Obstacles	**Executives Supplied**
Lack of high tech education/knowledge	Corporate funds to educate foreign students & foreign workers
No access to US high tech jobs	Forced Americans to train foreign workers taking their jobs
No access to US research projects	Foreign access to US research projects
Hard for foreign spy to get picture of even one proprietary product design	Foreign access to design databases storing drawings & bills of materials
Legal obstacles protecting US intellectual property	Foreign access to US intellectual property
Need to find suppliers of strategic parts	Contacts to strategic parts vendors
Must establish sales channels	US sales force to sell foreign made products
Corporate business plans tightly guarded	Foreign access to corporate business plans
Money to build manufacturing facilities	Corporate money to build foreign facilities
No access to future US design innovations	Foreign access to new US designs
Need operating capital	Corporate money to subsidize foreign operations
US Government trade protections	Lobbies to get US laws passed that gave tax incentives to offshore

Outsourcing Risks of Software Espionage

Highly skilled and experienced US IT professionals were the main obstacles to foreign espionage of our corporate databases. Once these Americans were laid off, under the guise of outsourcing "cost savings," the door was wide open. Foreign programmers have no loyalty to the US. Often they are underpaid, overworked, and therefore high risk. [45]

Executives outsourced maintaining proprietary software tools that had cost millions of dollars to develop. These customized software tools were created to refine product designs or manufacturing processes. Imagine the temptation for an outsourcing company. They can make far more money from secretly copying and selling this valuable software illegally to a competitor than they can from just maintaining the code. Non-disclosed negotiations meant there was little risk of being caught.

Executives also gave outsourcing companies insider *access to engineering computers storing confidential product design secrets* worth hundreds of millions of dollars. The product designs are worth many times the amount being paid for outsourcing services to maintain and enter data. [78] Again the foreign espionage temptation was great, and the chance of being caught minimal.

High tech US companies in Silicon Valley were ripe with strategic US technology secrets stored in computers. A "Regional Advantage" study explained that when people in a network needed help with "*anything*" they could "*pull data off of someone's computer down the street.*" [128] If the data being pulled was owned by different American companies, then copying and distributing the data would be stealing intellectual property. Were they supplying foreign competitors with stolen designs? Executives should not have given foreign access to strategic US computer systems.

Justice for Americans and America

Espionage in today's corporations is magnitudes beyond any espionage of the past. Only an insider in a position of power and trust could do this much damage.

Executives deceived Americans who thought they were investing in America and buying products and services produced by Americans. These executives knew what they were doing was wrong. That is why they cloaked their actions in secrecy.

There must be some legal remedy for American workers and investors harmed when executives offshored.

Chapter 5

Economic War on America

"Free trade" = We pay for it and other nations get it for free.

Throughout our history the US has engaged in global trade. Founders of our nation purchased items that they needed, and sold American products to other countries. Given that global trade has been engaged in from the founding of our nation, then what is "globalization"?

Some economists mistakenly assume that globalization is a product of *free trade* and that it will ultimately be beneficial to the US. If anyone questions globalization, foreign nations sound the alarm of protectionism. [167]

Globalization is not about *free-trade.*

Globalization is foreign workers and foreign companies being subsidized by foreign governments unfairly competing against US workers and businesses. Globalization is foreign governments paying "incentives" to US corporate executives to "transfer" our jobs and technology offshore. Globalization is "contributions" paid to US politicians to get outsourcing and offshoring legislation passed. [63]

A truly global economy would have been created by foreign countries developing their own technology and building their own companies from the ground up, to then compete and trade with us.

US Companies Lured to Offshore R&D

Foreign visa workers allowed to work in America learned our job skills and technology. This paved the way for offshoring: *"Once the knowledge transfer takes place, the offshoring begins."* [275]

Surprisingly, our government was not tracking the US jobs, US technology, and US capital investments 'transferred' offshore to foreign nations. Our leaders are dangerously relying on projections and impact statements made by promoters of offshoring. Instead, they should have been seeking objective data, and evaluating risks inherent in offshoring. [88]

"USA: Slowdown Sending Tech Jobs Overseas," a 2002 article reported corporations were accelerating offshoring to China, India, Ireland, and the Philippines to cut costs. It named high tech companies (*Boeing, Oracle, Cisco Systems, HP, and Microsoft*), financial companies (*Visa International, Citigroup, and Bank of America*), and retail (*Target, Gap and Nordstrom*). [105]

A 2004 *Economist* magazine survey found US companies planned big investments to set up R&D in China. At the same time *these companies planned to spend far less on R&D in our country. Moreover, they planned to spend* almost as much setting up R&D in India as in the US. [484] These executives were 'transferring' our technology leadership from the US to Asia.

India was luring strategic R&D from the US according to a 2006 article "Invented in India." For example, <u>Motorola spent $85 million to set up a research lab in India.</u> In turn the lab partnered with IIT and the Indian Institute of Science to do research on fuel cells and nano-emissive displays. Other big American companies named by the article that were setting up R&D in India included *IBM, Microsoft and Oracle. US companies also outsourced research to Indian companies including Infosys Technologies, Tata Consultancy Services, Wipro Technologies and more.* [598]

Downward Descent for American Corporations

US corporations enticed into outsourcing and offshoring spawned foreign competition. Ultimately, if this theft of jobs and technology is not reversed, our Government will no longer be a leading world power. And, our children will be at the mercy of countries who have stolen their inheritance.

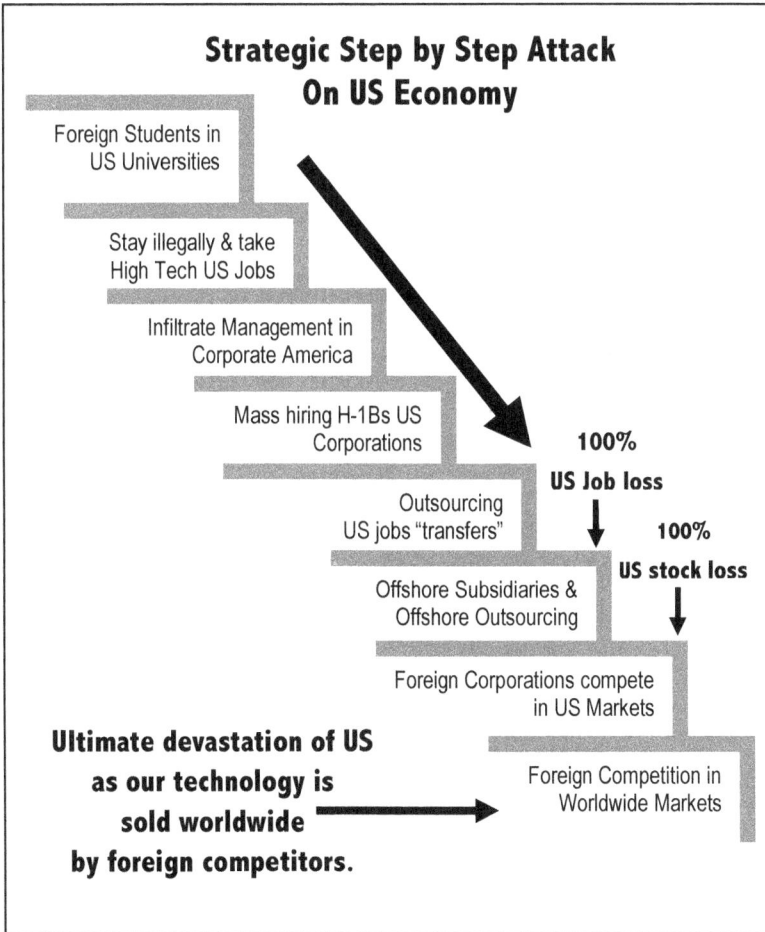

Strategic Step by Step Attack On US Economy

Foreign Students in US Universities

Stay illegally & take High Tech US Jobs

Infiltrate Management in Corporate America

Mass hiring H-1Bs US Corporations

100%

US Job loss

Outsourcing US jobs "transfers"

100%

US stock loss

Offshore Subsidiaries & Offshore Outsourcing

Foreign Corporations compete in US Markets

Ultimate devastation of US as our technology is sold worldwide by foreign competitors.

Foreign Competition in Worldwide Markets

Globalization's Hidden Costs

Outsourcing management of strategic engineering and financial computer systems can only be done if an American corporation trusts the outsourcer with confidential business information. When the outsourcing partner is foreign owned or offshore the risks of espionage go up exponentially. [76]

"Mergers, Economic Espionage, China, called Key IT Issues," was a 2006 article. It quoted FBI special agent Peter J. Ahearn who said, *"Once you go overseas, you can basically forget about intellectual property rights. You have to realize the intelligence services in foreign countries want the information you have, including intellectual property."* [945]

When US companies offshore to a foreign nation they are outside the protection of US laws. Offshoring gives foreigners access to computers storing patent ideas and research of American scientists and engineers. Not surprisingly, foreign countries providing outsourcing services began making leaps in bounds in technology and filing patent applications. [101] Do executives really expect a foreign country that is profiting from stealing US technology to stop?

Compounding the damage, a foreign outsourcing firm may sell outsourcing services to several American manufacturers in the same industry. They can pick the best design features from each company's database to create superior products. Then they can claim to have the best engineers and programmers, when in reality they are selling stolen designs gleaned from multiple clients.

In 2004, University of Michigan professor CK Prahalad, *"a global management guru"* who was to co-chair the university's new India center, talked about how people were caught off guard by *"the rate at which China and India are acquiring a world-class technology base and the speed at which they are beating others."* [253] Note the key word here is *"acquiring."*

Because of global threats our government is compelled to spend much of our R&D budget on defense. [484] In contrast, countries profiting from offshoring are increasing their spending on commercial R&D. China is planning to increase its basic research budget by 200% over the next decade. [484]

In 2009, the SEC advocated that US companies adopt international accounting rules. However, *critics warned that changing accounting rules would expose the US to more financial corruption putting billions of dollars at risk*. United Technologies, an aeronautics manufacturer and US government contractor, said it had a worldwide team working on converting to the new rules. It claimed that 60% of its revenue came from selling to foreign countries. [712]

Offshoring to China and India made these two countries major consumers of oil. This increased competition for oil was not factored into the "cost savings" for offshoring. China became the second biggest oil consumer. China was reported to be importing about one third of its oil. In 2004 it was consuming 5.46 million barrels of oil per day. India had to import almost 70% of the 2 million barrels a day that it consumed. India expected to use 7.5 million barrels a day by 2025. [623] As a result our cost for oil soared. So, we paid for studies that determined oil in Africa could cut our dependence on Middle Eastern oil. However, China and India read the US studies and then rushed into Africa to buy the oil according to a 2004, article, "China India Fight for African Oil." [623] We need leaders who do not give away our research.

Globalization is like thinking you're stepping on the back of a turtle that will give you a safe ride across the sound and discovering instead you're being rapidly carried out to sea on the back of a hungry shark.

Business Recovery Model

Americans need to wake up before it is too late. We need a recovery model that streamlines the process of identifying and removing corrupt executives, reclaiming technology and jobs, and reestablishing protection from foreign access to technology and research essential to our economy and national defense.

The propaganda claims that "globalization" is tipping the scales to help balance economies worldwide. The US will drop and Asia will soar. However, *the United States never caused the poverty in Asia*. It was a caused by oppression and overpopulation. In the end, "globalization" is a scam that will collapse and fail. It will not only harm Americans, it will harm people around the world.

Just as in the emergency drills when they tell passengers to put on their own oxygen mask before they try to help someone next to them, we need to give top priority to getting Americans back to work. Before we can help other nations we must first restore our economy. If our country collapses we will not be able to help anyone.

Chapter 6

Using Our Universities Against

US

Our universities pose a dangerous loophole in our national security.

For national security purposes visitors from *"countries of concern,"* such as China, India, Russia and more, [247] were prohibited from acquiring knowledge about sensitive technologies while visiting the US. Moreover, the US Government Export Administration Regulations also barred the export of sensitive equipment and materials that could be used to create advanced military capabilities such as supercomputers, encryption tools, and nuclear and biological materials to *"countries of concern."*

However, there was a big loophole in our security. We locked the front door and windows, but we left the back door wide open. Our government exempted U.S. universities from the bans even though our government knew that *"foreign governments are targeting universities."* [247]

Just as we taught the 9/11 terrorists to fly our airplanes, despite repeated warnings our government granted millions of student visas to nations that our leaders knew pose IW threats.

Foreign nations used our universities to channel spies into our country. These spies then gained access to closely guarded military and commercial research.

Foreign Governments Target Our Universities

"American Universities Infected by Foreign Spies Detected by FBI," an April 2012 article on *bloomburg.com* quoted FBI assistant director for counterintelligence, Frank Figliuzzi:, "*We have intelligence and cases indicating that U.S. universities are indeed a target of foreign intelligence services.*" They found that in 2010 the Middle East doubled its US spying, and that *East Asia increased its spying by eightfold!* A former CIA officer said *China has over 3,000 front companies in our country, "for the sole purpose of acquiring our technology.*" And a senior fellow on Asian Military Affairs said that our universities enabled China "*to leapfrog into the cutting edge of military capability on the way to superpower status.*" [1001] As you read, you will see these warnings about "*front companies*" repeated earlier warnings given in 1997, and again in 2005.

Foreign governments told spies to befriend US professors, and tried to *recruit Americans studying abroad to become spies.* [1001] Some university leaders cooperated with the FBI. However, others did not. For example, Stanford President John Hennessy testified at a 2010 congressional hearing: "*Stanford does not, nor will it, restrict participation of students on the basis of citizenship.*" Over half of Stanford's graduate students in engineering and physical science were foreign. Congressman Dana Rohrabacher asked Hennessy if he knew that China sent students to the US to gather military intelligence. Hennessy replied, "*I am aware of that.*" Rohrabacher admonished that our universities need to be patriotic. [1001]

"Education Needs in Iraq," a 2010 article in Virginia Tech's College of Business Magazine reported that due to war embargos "*all faculty (in Iraq) have been cut off from newer technologies, equipment, research and academic collaboration for years.*" So, Virginia Tech sent faculty to Iraq because "*There is also a great need for Iraqi faculty to visit our universities to update their knowledge and skills.*" Iraqi universities wanted to know about US advances in "*nano-technology, genetic engineering and biotechnology...*" [1005]

Using Our Universities to Spy

Years of warnings about foreign governments using students to spy were ignored. As mentioned earlier, Berkowitz's War in the Information Age book in 1995 cautioned: "*A more subtle alternative might be to send several hundred promising students to school to become computer experts and covert hackers.*" [420]

"Rethinking Foreign Students: A Question of National Interest," warned in 2002 that *our universities educated foreign students from "countries of concern" in high risk subjects including: nuclear chemistry, organic chemistry, chemical engineering, nuclear engineering and nuclear physics, and more.* [230]

In 2004 a report, "Foreign Students in the United States," by the Federation for American Immigration Reform claimed *scientists working on India's and Iran's nuclear and biological weapons research got their training in our universities.* [252]

The Director of the FBI testified to Congress in 2004 that, "*Some Foreign governments ask foreign students specifically to acquire information on a variety of subjects and upon the completion of their studies, some foreign students are then encouraged to seek employment with US firms to steal proprietary information.*" And, the Deputy Director of the FBI testified: "*We know for a fact that organizations funded by a state sponsor of terrorism fund students coming to the United States. And that is part of their intelligence organization.*" [252]

Some Chinese students in high tech fields such as computer science were in reality foreign spies according to a 2000 article on americavisas.com. Many were even related to Communist party officials. In other cases "*real students are ordered to report what they learn about U.S. high tech research to the Chinese government.*" Despite the dangers, Chinese students were given access to advanced computers at our National Weapons Laboratories. [246] In 2011, a record number of 157,588 student visas were granted to students from China. [983]

Globally Competitive Strategy Reality Check

The Council of Graduate Schools in 2005 claimed it is imperative that foreign students do research to keep us globally competitive. [477] Since the 1950's foreign student visas increased 2000% hitting record levels. In 2011 over 700,000 came.

If it were true that foreign students doing research made the United States globally competitive, then our technology leadership would have been growing by leaps and bounds. However, just the opposite was occurring. *The foreign nations supplying these foreign students were rapidly acquiring US technology which is more indicative of foreign spying or "knowledge transfer."*

Look Who's Getting Our University Research

Job losses to foreign workers depleted the amount of money our government and businesses had to invest in research. Guess who picked up the slack? *Our government allowed foreign owned companies to "invest" in US University R&D.*

For example, India's Tata Consultancy Services (TCS), a foreign outsourcing company, spent around $3.5 million in 2005 to sponsor R&D funding at prestigious US schools such as MIT and Carnegie Mellon. In return Tata *can "walk away with whatever intellectual property is created."* Although it finances research centers in India, TCS used its access to our universities to *"leverage the innovation infrastructure in the U.S."* [484] Tata will own US patents invented in our universities!

Why does Tata feel a need to tap into our universities and our students when propaganda claims that India's IIT is superior to our universities, and students from India are brighter than American students? The president of Tata's US subsidiary admitted that they were *"not seeing enough innovation from the Indian companies."* [484]

From Aid to Raid

In the 1970's and 1980's India, Taiwan, and China channeled large numbers of students into our university graduate programs. These foreign students were funded by US aid to create goodwill ambassadors. Instead, they stayed in our country illegally after they graduated. At first it was a trickle. It soon grew into a river. Then it became a flood. *They kept a low profile. As illegal aliens they used predatory pricing to take Americans' jobs.* Executives inflated their bonuses by hiring these illegal, college educated workers at below job market rates.

The longer they stayed in the US, the less they perceived their risk of deportation. They boldly began to press for amnesty. The 1986 amnesty gave hundreds of thousands of student visa violators US citizenship.

Once legal, they came out of the shadows. They became professors in our universities, executives in our corporations, and got jobs in our government agencies. Next, many of them persuaded US executives to falsely testify to Congress that our country had a "desperate" shortage of high tech workers. *Only four years after getting amnesty, they got Congress to pass H-1B legislation in 1990 that allowed foreign student graduates to 'legally' seek jobs in the US.* [47]

Instead of melding with Americans, many formed racially divisive networks that played a key role in transferring US technology, jobs, and money to their countries of origin. [372]

- *Taiwanese engineers living in Silicon Valley formed the "Monte Jade Science and Technology Association" in 1990.*

- *People from India living in Silicon Valley formed "The Indus Entrepreneurs" (TiE) network in 1992.*

- *The Chinese started the Hua Yuan Science and Technology Association in 1999.* [512]

Efforts to Shore up Security Thwarted

The Defense Advanced Research Projects Agency (DARPA), and the National Science Foundation (NFS) and other agencies rely heavily on university research. *Our tax dollars are funding military research on security, communications, combat robots, biological risks, decision support systems, aeronautics, satellite surveillance, and more.* [621]

When our government realized the university exemptions for access to sensitive technologies were dangerous, it met with stiff resistance when it tried to close this security loophole.

In 2000, our Government wanted to require university staff working on Department of Defense (DOD) projects to submit to background checks. A university Vice Provost for Research objected because national security clearance checks could only be run on US citizens. Research administrators at the University of California wrote a memo incredulously protesting that it was *"unacceptable" to restrict access to our defense research based on citizenship.* [247] (Also read about the foreign takeover of our graduate schools in the book False Prophets of False Profits.)

There were also protests when our government wanted to restrict DOD sponsored conferences to university employees who signed Critical Technical Data Agreements. These contracts can only be signed by US citizens and permanent US residents. [246]

In October 2004, our government wanted to require that foreign students and scientists from *"countries of concern"* obtain a license from the US Department of Commerce prior to operating lab equipment. They were blocked by college administrators. [247]

US universities argued that foreign student graduates should stay in the US because *sending them back to their own country would create economic and security threats.* [621] So, if they knew this education was dangerous, why were they recruiting foreign students?

"India Abroad" Interns in Congress

In 1994, *India Abroad* set up an "Indian American Center for Political Awareness" (IACPA) with offices in Washington DC. IACPA then started the Washington Leadership Program (WLP) to place Indian interns inside US Congressional offices.

In a ten year period IACPA managed to place over 150 interns in our nation's capital. IACPA also arranged special meetings for interns to connect with *"political Diaspora"* in our federal, state, and local agencies. [425]

Troublingly, WLP also sent interns to India. [425] An intern returning from India in 2004 commented, *"listening to the great Montek Singh Ahluwali, Deputy Chairman of the Planning Commission, I often was in awe that we were <u>in India on a trip to meet its highest political officials</u>. Yet, throughout* the trip *I was amazed that every politician, diplomat, justice, minister or NGO official that we met with took stock in our opinions and <u>said that they learned much by meeting with us</u>."*[425]

This raises several red flags. Our government officials may not feel a need for discretion and protection of confidential documents around interns. What more dangerous and ominous a spy than one planted as an eager to learn intern by a foreign government right in the midst of US government offices. [425]

The IACPA website section on "Political Awareness," defines hate crimes as: "Crimes that are motivated by race, religion, or country of origin." In particular H.R. 80 bill that would elevate *"crimes based on race, color, or religion or national origin to Federal offenses. ...The bill also makes it a crime for an adult to recruit a juvenile for the purposes of hate motivated crimes."* [425] They want the bill to benefit their "community." Yet, *did they travel to India and provide inside information on our government to a foreign government based on race, color, religion, or country of origin?* These interns were the same age as our soldiers fighting and dying in Iraq and Afghanistan.

Our Universities Lured Offshore to Asia!

Some US universities offer online degrees to students in foreign countries. [615] India and China are the two main beneficiaries. Here's a big surprise–China and India also lured US universities to build brick and mortar branches in their countries.

US UNIVERSITIES IN CHINA!

US university presidents signed deals with Chinese universities even though it is not profitable and they struggled to breakeven on expenses. If these deals are not profitable, then someone is paying. Are young American college students paying high tuition to fund building US university branches in China? Moreover, they signed these "deals" despite the economic and national security risks and diplomatic tensions between the US and China.

In June 2005, several US university presidents joined in a forum held in Seattle, Washington. Their agenda was to build educational ties with China. Some US universities, such as Arizona State University, Stanford, Yale, MIT and others had already sent faculty to teach in China. [532] Are the faculty members traveling to China working on confidential commercial or defense research?

US UNIVERSITIES IN INDIA!

India was even more aggressive than China. For example, in 2001, MIT's US Media Lab Executive Director acknowledged *the lab was in negotiations with the government of India to build a lab in India bigger than the lab in the United States.* The government of India was expected to pay only about 20% of the cost. [262]

In 2004, Indian professors, M.S. Krishnan and C.K. Prahalad, persuaded the *University of Michigan to setup a research center at the Indian Institute of Information Technology in Bangalore, India.* The University was to arrange for US faculty and students to take trips to India and work on research projects. [253]

In 2005, _our high tech companies, universities, and research centers collaborated to provide educational and research opportunities in India_. The absurd justification was that foreign students comprised almost 58% of the PhD candidates in US engineering classes. Again, India was expected to cover only 20% of the costs.

Parties to the agreement:

- _US high tech companies including Microsoft, Qualcomm, Cadence Design, and more agreed to provide financing._

- _US universities: UC Berkley, UC San Diego, Carnegie Mellon University, Cornell University, Case Western Reserve University, and New York State University Buffalo agreed to encourage faculty on sabbaticals to teach advanced technology courses in engineering, computer science, communication technologies, biotechnology, bioinformatics, nanotechnology, medical sciences, and more._

- _US research centers included University of California's Centre for Information Technology Research in the Interest of Society, the California Institute for Telecommunications and Information Technology, and Carnegie Mellon's CyLab._ [241]

Restore US University Patriotism

We need to do a serious revamping of our universities to assure they promote and protect our national interests. Our universities should not be hotbeds for terrorists and spies. We fund our universities to keep our nation globally competitive and to shore up our national defense. _Universities that weaken our competitiveness, and jeopardize our national security violate their charter to serve our country._

We need to carefully screen and reduce the number of foreign students and professors, and _to limit what they can access._ Our universities betray our country when they harbor and educate foreign spies. _Defense research needs to be done by Americans loyal to our nation. Otherwise, we may be safer not to do the research at all._

Chapter 7

Information Warfare

Then: "The pen is mightier than the sword"

Now: The computer is mightier than the missile.

Information is power. In times of war, the course of history has been altered by an intercepted letter or document. For example, in WWII breaking the Enigma Code used by the Germans was a key factor helping us win the war.

Because of H-1B visas, outsourcing, and offshoring, foreign workers can do much more than intercept one letter or document. Many work on our computer systems where they can monitor and record email, phone calls, phone records, computer files, and more.

It is dangerous to employ foreign workers in our communications companies that have the ability to *"wiretap and data-mine Americans' communications."* In 2006, a civil liberties group filed a lawsuit against AT&T for working with the US National Security Administration (NSA). The lawsuit questioned our government's right to spy. [493]

If a telecom company can help our government spy, then it or one of its employees can help a foreign government spy. Alarmingly, Bruce Berkowitz's 1995 book, <u>War in the Information Age</u> reported that almost 95% of US military communications use commercial lines, and that US companies were offshoring production of microchips used in our military aircraft and weapons. [420]

H-1B Linked to Foreign Espionage

Congress failed to consider that passing the H-1B visa legislation deprived young US citizens the opportunity to develop strategic software skills for our military, and discouraged them from pursuing computer science degrees.

Additionally, during the dotcom boom, foreign venture capital launched large numbers of startups that drew many experienced American programmers away from strategic jobs in our defense industry. One large aerospace firm lost 37% of its programmers. This created a dangerous shortage of programmers within our Department of Defense. [38] Foreign nations knew exactly what they were doing–they had H-1Bs chomping at the bit to fill these highly sensitive US government jobs.

"A California Reader Draws the Connection between Heavy H-1B Usage and Corporate Fraud, Big Financial Losses," post on *VDare.com* lamented that *"the general public continues to be blissfully unaware of the economic and security threats posed by the H-1B visa program."* [718] He observed companies that employed H-1Bs such as *Enron, WorldCom,* and *Tyco* suffered big financial losses, technical breakdowns, and legal trouble. And, he warned H-1Bs were programming our voting machines. [206]

In *early 2001, two H-1Bs from China that were working at Lucent were charged with industrial espionage.* [23] *By 2002, H-1Bs had infiltrated jobs in* "some of our most sensitive industries and so have the potential for setting up terrorist activities." [53]

Most H-1Bs who engaged in foreign espionage will never be caught because they were given insider access. An estimated 85% of the corporate intellectual property theft was done by insiders. *For foreign spies prized targets were high-tech companies (R&D), followed by manufacturing and our service industries.* [202]

Foreign Espionage Costs Us Billions

Foreign programmers were given insider access to our computers storing our university research, technology secrets, and even proprietary government computer systems.

In 1997, foreign espionage was estimated to have stolen more than $300 billion worth of US intellectual property. The FBI reported that over 100 nations engaged in espionage against US companies. By 1998, more than 90% of our Fortune 500 computer systems had been hacked. [202]

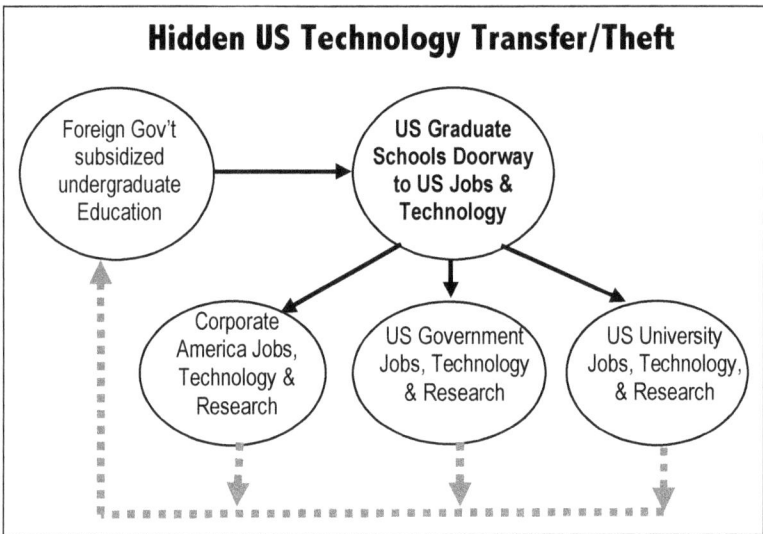

Hidden US Technology Transfer/Theft

Foreign Gov't subsidized undergraduate Education

US Graduate Schools Doorway to US Jobs & Technology

Corporate America Jobs, Technology & Research

US Government Jobs, Technology & Research

US University Jobs, Technology, & Research

In 2002, Global Software Competitiveness Studies sounded the alarm: *"When it comes to software and security, our nation's leaders are ignorant."* We were in a catch-22, dependent on our government to protect us, when it was foreign student visa and H-1B visa legislation passed by Congress that made us vulnerable in the first place. [200]

Outsourcing National Security!

Our leaders moved confidential government systems onto the Internet, while at the same time they deployed our Internet technology to foreign nations. As a result, in 1995 alone there were <u>250,000 known cyber attacks on Department of Defense (DOD) computers</u>. An alarming 65% were successful! [202] But 250,000 was just the elephants tracks; for each attack caught, thousands may go undetected.

After 9/11 Bush appointed Tom Ridge to head Homeland Security. An *informationweek.com* article said Ridge as a "<u>barely PC literate</u>" governor had JNet ("*a network to let federal law-enforcement, defense and intelligence agencies collaborate.*") developed by *KPMG a big employer of H-1Bs, and Tata an India outsourcing company. Even worse he <u>became the first governor to outsource data centers</u>!* [207] [205]

Our Department of Defense in 2002 wanted to stop employing foreign nationals as contractors in computer jobs processing paychecks, inventorying supplies, and <u>email</u>. The Department of Justice and Department of Treasury had already implemented similar protections. [203] *A CNN story warned that the US suffers from a "<u>tech-illiterate leadership in Washington.</u>"* Our DOD slogan, "Military superiority through information superiority" [226] is ridiculous if our IT jobs go to foreign workers. Instead of cutting back, outsourcing accelerated! "Outsourcing the Pentagon: Who's Winning the Big Contracts," a 2004 article reported large DOD contracts were outsourced to: *Lockheed Martin, Boeing, Raytheon, General Dynamics, Northrop Grumman, United Technologies, General Electric, and Newport News.* [442] *How many employ foreign workers which instead of building up our defenses may be endangering us?!*

"When you send an email...that email can traverse the world...It leaves imprints at several locations and could potentially be used to reconstruct the email, even if you deleted the email," said VA Tech professor Rajesh Bagchi in 2012. [1064] *So, why didn't General Petraeus, Director of our CIA, know emails are not secure? He was so tech-illiterate he wrote emails to his mistress! <u>What else did he write in emails?!</u>*

Government Contractors Outsource & Offshore

Our private sector owns and controls our nation's infrastructure systems. [209] So, our government had to partner with US telecom companies, and financial services companies to try to secure our infrastructure. [208] The problem with this strategy is that these *"partners" are the very ones who displaced Americans with foreign workers.*

But that is not all; many corporations awarded government contracts offshored the work or hired offshore subcontractors. Our state and federal governments were not tracking government work being channeled offshore. For example in 2001 United Technologies, a US military contractor, made it a goal to offshore 80% of its software application and support to India. [6] Finally, in 2002, our government began to collect data to learn the extent of government work being sent offshore. [105]

Corruption in companies receiving government contracts abounds. Some of the biggest federal contractors had enforcement cases that involved *breaking US export laws, failure to disclose financial data to the government, and even actions that put the US national security at risk.* These companies had to pay billions in fines to our government. Still a small group of about 40 companies got $4 out of every $10 federal dollars spent on procurement. [135]

Despite the dangers, offshoring continued under the Bush Administration. India protested any protections and was reassured by Bush that if he was reelected in 2004 outsourcing and offshoring would continue–he was reelected and offshoring got much worse.

After much damage was done, our business and political leaders began to realize that offshoring jeopardized our national security. Gartner, a research firm, reported in 2005 that *"concerns about job losses will be <u>overshadowed by these security issues</u>."* [201]

Cyber Threat Like a "Well-Placed Bomb"

It is hard to catch cyber attackers, so there is little to deter them. Information Warfare (IW) capabilities can be obtained more quickly and cheaply than airplanes, tanks and bombs. There are two basic kinds of cyber attacks. First there are attacks that seek to disrupt computer systems. Second are attacks that are aimed at stealing valuable information.

Cyber attacks on our federal agencies jumped from 5,500 in 2006 to 16,800 in 2008, according to an article, "Pentagon Cyber Command to Create force for Digital Warfare." And, under the Obama *cyber attacks against our Defense Department computers doubled in the spring of 2009.* The Pentagon spent $100 Million repairing damage caused by cyber attacks. The Government Accountability Office's *"mantra"* was to spend more money. [957] Obama made "India-born" Vivek Kundra our nation's first Chief Information Officer to oversee federal computer systems.

In 2008 Rep. Frank Wolf (R-VA) who spoke out against human rights violations in China said hackers broke into his staff computers and stole information on political dissidents. A story about the incident, "Rep. Wolf: China Hacked Congressional Computers," reported that he was troubled at our government's *"apparent lack of a sense of national urgency"* with cyber breaches.

In 2010, "FBI Warns Brewing Cyberwar May Have Same Impact as 'Well-Placed Bomb'," reported that FBI Director Robert Mueller warned that *foreign governments were using hackers to steal our business and military technologies and strategies.* [952]

"Biggest National Security Threat: Cyber Attack," another 2010 report found: *"Key American computer networks are attacked thousands of times a day.... the truth is, we aren't doing enough to stop it."* Foreign governments sponsored hackers. We spent a fortune on cyber security, yet we were in more danger than before. It said we must *"Grant the president new emergency powers."* [956]

Sophisticated Clandestine Cyber Attacks

"Cyber-attack on U.S. Firms, Google Traced to Chinese," a March 2010 *washingtontimes.com* article reported on a well-planned "sophisticated" and "targeted" cyber attack. Gary Elliott, a cyber-warfare specialist, said: *"There was a large government military or intelligence agency behind this."* [962] How they did it:

1) *First attackers found a hole in the Internet Explorer browser to exploit.*

2) *Next they gathered insider information on targeted US Companies' computer networks learning where important data was stored and identified the executives who had high level access.*

3) *Then the "executives who had high-level access" were studied for months gathering their personal data from MySpace, Facebook, Linked In, and Twitter —all to learn who they trusted.*

4) *Finally, cyber-attackers sent an email or instant message to each executive and made it appear to be from a trusted friend. Clicking on the email linked the victim's computer to a server in Taiwan that downloaded software "that allowed attackers to take over the computer." Victims thought their computer was protected by firewalls, but the "trap-door software" had the victim's own computer reach out beyond the firewall to make the connection.*

5) *Alarmingly attackers may have planted "undetectable software on American company networks that could allow further clandestine access or even total control of computers in the future."* [962]

We are in a dangerously vulnerable position. A March 2012 *Fox News* report, "Retiring FBI Official Says current Cyber Security Strategy 'Unsustainable'," quoted Shawn Henry, an FBI assistant director in charge of cyber security, who said hackers could easily get around our government and businesses security to steal sensitive data. He said the current methods *"never get ahead, never become secure, never have a reasonable expectation of privacy or security."* [999]

Need to Limit Foreign Access to US Computers

Some of the most critical high tech jobs during war today are computer programming, microprocessor chips, communications, and biotechnology. By channeling these jobs to foreigners, executives are endangering US national security. It is vital that these jobs go to US citizens loyal to our country. [63]

There are some applications that should not be on the Internet. Moving our infrastructure to the Internet was unnecessary. Now online computer systems control our electric power grids, our chemical plant processes, our emergency systems, our water distribution, and more. Many networks are interrelated. An attack on one system could ripple through and cause damage to other systems. [204]

In April 2004, Tom Daschle introduced a Bill that would have required US companies to reveal to Congress the number of jobs they planned to offshore. *Introduction of this bill angered executives and foreign companies who "*have gone out of their way to hide the number of jobs being moved to India*."* [93] A few months after stepping on the toes of India's offshore juggernaut Daschle lost his 2004 reelection bid to the Senate. Was there a hidden connection?

In contrast, after his Homeland Security job, Ridge was a marquee speaker for Covits 2005, "The Promise of Digital Government" that *promoted outsourcing government IT work*. Sponsors included: MCI, Nortel, Cisco Systems, Oracle, Sun Microsystems, Microsoft, EDS, Accenture, Novell, Gartner and more. Most, if not all, hired H-1Bs and outsourced. [409]

We need some tech savvy Americans in Congress who understand that our computers and software need to be produced in America by Americans. And, they should be Americans that have warned about giving H-1Bs and other foreign workers access to our government and business computers.

Chapter 8

China Spy Network

Betrayed by new immigrants!

Proponents of mass immigration to the United States, fail to acknowledge that many of the new immigrants have foreign government agendas. Most disconcerting is how they may live among us for many years as fellow Americans who swore allegiance to our country.

"China's Huge Spy Network in U.S." a 2005 article alleged that China is *using stolen US technology secrets to build a war machine that threatens the US and the rest of the world.* According to the article a pentagon security director warned: "*China has somewhere between 2,000 and 3,000 front companies in the U.S., and their sole reason for existing is to steal, exploit technology.*" [199]

Harry Wu, a Chinese dissident who had been forced to work in a Chinese slave labor camp said China was flooding the US with "Made in China" products to fund China's military buildup. He pointed out the fallacy of thinking that trade would turn China into a democracy. He warned that just because China was making a lot of money it did not mean an end to Communist oppression. The article laments the lack of media coverage of how outsourcing funds the dangerous growth of China's military: "*The problem has received scant mention in the mainstream media. So millions of Americans are blissfully unaware of it.*" [199]

How many spies gained US citizenship through the 1986 amnesty? Following are a few examples of spies that were caught.

Spies Caught Stealing Microprocessor Designs

In 2001, Fei Ye a 40 year old engineer from China who had been granted US citizenship, and Ming Zhong a 39 year old engineer from China who had been granted a green card both pleaded guilty to two counts of "*economic espionage to benefit a foreign country.*" [576]

They were arrested at the San Francisco International Airport attempting to board a flight to China with "*thousands of pages of trade secrets stolen from four Silicon Valley companies -- NEC, Sun Microsystems, Transmeta Corp., and Trident Microsystems Inc.*" stowed away in their luggage. They planned to startup a microprocessor company with $2 million in funding from two cities in China. Other documents seized at their houses included a business plan to advance "*China's stature in the field of integrated circuit design,*" and, a review by Chinese government officials that liked their plan and "encouraged agencies to provide financial support." [576]

Spy Caught Stealing Military Technologies

In 2006, Xiaodong Sheldon Meng a 42 year old Chinese engineer was charged with attempting to sell Silicon Valley trade secrets to Asian governments. In 2008, Meng pleaded guilty to two felonies, "*economic espionage,*" and "*exporting controlled military technologies.*" He was only sentenced to 24 months when he could have gotten 25 years. His sentence was criticized as "*ridiculously light*" for the espionage he committed. [576] [960]

Spy Wanted to "Contribute to the Motherland"

Dongfan Chung a 72 year old "*naturalized US citizen, was indicted ... on espionage, conspiracy and obstructing justice charges*" of stealing national defense aerospace information from defense contractor Boeing where he had worked. The Justice Department reported that it had a letter Chung wrote that he was spying to "*contribute to the motherland.*" [669]

Spy caught Stealing National Defense Information

In 2008, the Justice Department reported that 58 year old Tai Kuo a naturalized US citizen born in Taiwan, was *"charged with conspiracy to deliver national defense information to a foreign government."* Kuo was caught on tape "chuckling" about his spy activities. [669]

A May 2011 *CBS News* story reported Kuo came to our country on a non-immigrant student visa in 1973. He was skilled at networking and gaining people's trust, so China recruited him as a spy. Why did he betray us? He admitted *"Just pure and simple greed."* After he was caught, he pleaded guilty. Most disturbing is the fact that he was viewed as *"a shining immigrant success story,"* living among us over 30 years. An ex-friend denounced him as *"worse than a thief...a traitor."* Kuo was *"one of dozens convicted in the last three years of efforts to pass secrets or restricted technology to the Chinese."* [961]

Spy from India Sold US Military Secrets to China

Now here's an interesting twist: a 67 year old immigrant from India was convicted by a federal jury in 2010 for selling US military stealth missile secrets to China so that he could pay the mortgage on his multimillion dollar ocean view home. Noshir Gowadia came to our country on a non-immigrant student visa in the 1960's. It wasn't until almost 10 years later that he was granted US citizenship. Did he break our immigration laws and stay illegally when he completed his studies? He worked at Northrop until 1986, and then became a consultant.

The *USA Today* article, "U.S. Engineer Convicted of Selling Secrets to China," said Gowadia's case *"is one of a series of major prosecutions targeting alleged Chinese spying on the U.S."* [953] Again we have what would have been cited as a glowing example of immigration success where he had been living among us as a fellow American for well over 30 years when he was caught betraying us. Had he been betraying our country for years, and this was the first time he was caught?

Chapter 9

"Asian Miracle Model"

Then: Low cost component supplier.

Now: High tech competitor.

Recall the opening line in *The Times of India* story in the first chapter celebrated: "*The rise of China and India as global players is heralding an Asian Century in place of a receding American Century, a US intelligence report said on Thursday.*" [405]

The key to understanding how the rise of Asia is causing a decline in America is the "Asian Miracle Model" described in a 2008 article: "India Rides Growth Wave Into New Age of Tech Globalization." It said India was following the *"historic three-wave model"* that was used by *Japan, South Korea, Southeast Asia, and China.*

The "Asian Miracle" model's first wave is luring American companies to offshore component production to take advantage of cheap labor. Once entrenched, they begin *"moving up the value chain."* Wave two; they persuade American companies to offshore manufacturing the products that are built using the components such as computers. The lure for wave two is to claim Asia provides huge market opportunities. Then the big third wave is a destructive tsunami. In this wave Asian companies create their own knock-off brands to market globally, and compete head on against the American companies that offshored and entrusted technology and business secrets to them. [673]

India played the model to the hilt to become the "hub" for "*a turning point in the shift of industry's balance of power from West to East.*" In Wave 1 India sold IT outsourcing to US companies for maintaining low level software code.

Then for Wave 2, India "moved up the value chain" to gain access to American companies' databases containing technology secrets. India was quite successful in luring US companies including: Oracle, IBM, Cisco, Microsoft, Sun Microsystems and more. For example, IBM hired 76,000 employees in India, and "*IBM has put India at the apex of its global IT strategy.*"

Then India's wave 3 struck at the heart of our IT industry forging IT partnerships with China, Egypt, Pakistan, Australia, and Dubai. [673]

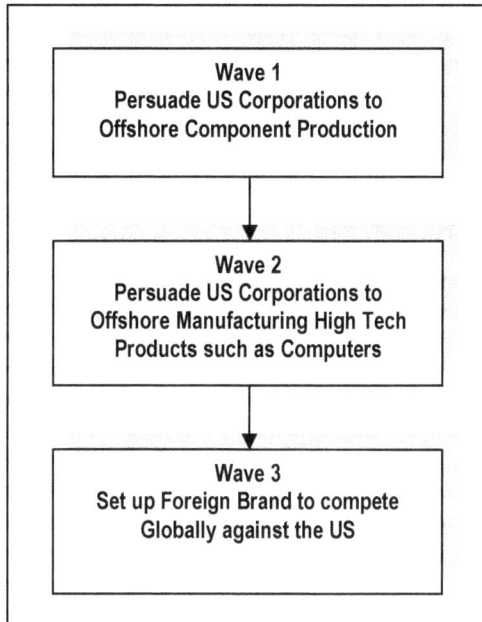

Wave 1
Persuade US Corporations to
Offshore Component Production

Wave 2
Persuade US Corporations to
Offshore Manufacturing High Tech
Products such as Computers

Wave 3
Set up Foreign Brand to compete
Globally against the US

Outsourcing Wolf

Outsourcing's honey-toned promises were like the wolf in granny's bed and hat speaking welcoming words all the while luring Little Red Riding Hood closer so that he could devour her.

American corporations were lured one by one to offshore to India and China by promises of huge market opportunities. The companies that were ravaged covered up their losses instead of warning others. Our media also failed to warn US companies about the dangers of offshoring to Asia. *US companies that thought they were going for a picnic soon discovered they were the picnic for the outsourcing wolf.* Many US companies did not survive, and most of the others were badly injured. [300]

The perils of investing in China were detailed in an article "China's Hunger for Knowledge." It explained how China lured high tech US companies with promises of huge market opportunities. The baited company would pay millions of dollars to build and equip operations in China under the illusion that big profits would soon follow. Next, China coerced US executives into revealing our technology secrets and into training Chinese workers. *Ultimately, US executives discovered the Chinese government had subversively used them to set up state sponsored competitors that not only competed against them in the Chinese market but in the global market as well.* [164] Why were they silent—were they blackmailed?

This pattern was repeated over and over. Despite the threat to intellectual property, hundreds of US companies gave in to China's demands—including US companies that *sell dual use, commercial and military use, technologies.* [173] For example, in the 1990's McDonnell Douglas Corporation, a US manufacturer of commercial and military planes, jumped into the Chinese market expecting huge revenues. To get into the market, they agreed to train Chinese workers to assemble planes. Critics said this dangerously *"involved one of the largest technology transfers in history."* [173]

Asian-Silicon Valley Connection (ASVC)

The Asian-Silicon Valley Connection (ASVC) forum wrote: "*The world has tremendous interest in Silicon Valley because of its success in the technology sector and wealth creation.*" ASVC sponsors were *IBM, Cisco, Yahoo, Ernst & Young*, and many more.

ASVC's goal is *to "promote Asian interests" through "networking between Silicon Valley and Asia" that "will reshape the global economy." ASVC claimed Asia was "on target to overtake the U.S. and Europe" in spending on information technology (IT).*

ASVC boasted that *33% of the CEO's in Silicon Valley are Asian,* and that *Asians hold over 50% of the high tech jobs in the Silicon Valley*, and that Silicon Valley has become a "*center of strong Asian influence.*" [643] These are shocking statistics for a group that demographically is only 1-3% of our population. They claimed: "*Silicon Valley and Asia, already inarguably the two most important technology regions in the world.*" [643] Silicon Valley yes; but, has Asia taken more than we know?

ASVC *acknowledged that American companies had lost billions of dollars trying to do business in Asia*. In October 2000, while our economy was reeling from the dotcom crash, ASVC held its "*first gala function in Palo Alto.*" It was attended by 600 executives and 70 venture capitalists. [643] Apparently while Americans were trying to bind up deep dotcom wounds, they were partying. A few of ASVC's Board members in 2007 included:

- *ASVC President, Vinie Zhang, born in Shanghai, MBA from the University of California at Berkeley. A VP in a venture capital firm that funded biotechnology, IT, and nano technology. She promoted funding startups in China.*

- *Tina Wang, born in Shanghai, China, advised US high tech companies on setting up subsidiaries in China.*

- *Vivien Wang employed by Deloitte & Touche LLP advised US companies on strategies for offshoring to China.* [643]

US Taxpayers "Made Silicon Valley"

Silicon Valley belongs to America, not Asia. In February 1999, the CEO of TechNet acknowledged that it was federal funds, i.e. our taxes that *"made Silicon Valley."* [184]

Back in the early 1970's, to *shore up our technology leadership in semiconductors, electronics, and more,* our taxes funded partnerships between universities and industry to *facilitate moving technology from US university research labs to US businesses.*

Networks developed where university researchers, business leaders, customers, suppliers and investors worked together. This collaboration gave birth to high tech networks in Silicon Valley and the Route 128 corridor close to Boston. For example, in 1973 the National Science Foundation (NSF) started the *Industry/University Cooperative Research Centers* (I/UCRCs). And, in 1979 the NSF launched its *Engineering Research Centers* (ERCs) program. The goals were to conduct technology research *vital to our nation's future and to train engineering leaders for the United States.* [185]

Our taxes funding federal research were very unevenly distributed. For example, in 1988 California received almost $44 billion of this R&D money *taking one out of every five dollars spent.* California universities and colleges received more R&D money than any other state in our country. California got more research money from the National Aeronautics and Space Administration (NASA) and from the National Science Foundation (NSF) than any other state. [171] This uneven distribution continued for many years. For example, in 2010 an NSF Award summary showed California received *$1 billion;* the next highest recipient was Massachusetts that got less than half that amount. [965]

We taxpayers are still making Silicon Valley. *Most Americans don't know Silicon Valley has been largely taken over by Asia.*

Stealth Takeover of Silicon Valley

How did India and China do a stealth takeover of Silicon Valley? In the 1970's and 1980's there was a wave of students from India and China we educated that got jobs as *engineers in the US defense and aerospace* programs during the Cold War. [618] By 1990 25% of the scientists and engineers employed in high tech jobs in California were foreign born! [372] [272] [310]

"Where Integrated Chip means Indians, Chinese," a 2000 *India Express* article claimed our *1990 US census found that immigrants in Silicon Valley took 32% of the science and engineering jobs. And, 74% of these immigrants came from China and India.* [330] The article lauded the "*stealth takeover*" of a quarter of US technology companies by immigrants from China and India from 1980-1999. [330]

The Chinese gained an iron grip on our hardware industry.

Immigrants from India stealthily took control of our software industry. *It said Microsoft has "dozens of Indians" in its upper management echelons, and hired so many people from India that it was nicknamed "Surya Microsystems."* [330]

The article went so far as to claim: *"When local technologists claim that Silicon Valley is built on ICs they refer not to the Integrated Circuit but to Indian and Chinese engineers."* [330]

It is false to claim that immigrants from India and China "built" Silicon Valley. Americans built high tech Silicon Valley. Americans Jack Kilby and Robert Noyce were the inventors of the integrated circuit (IC) in 1959. [406] The microprocessor was invented and patented by Ted Hoff, Jr. also an American in 1971. [407] According to the "Important Historical Inventions and Inventors" list published by the LSU Libraries, Americans were the inventors of our advanced technologies. [406]

Silicon Valley R&D Demographics

The H-1B "non-immigrant visa" changed the demographics of Silicon Valley. In 1998 Asians comprised 2% of the native born IT workers reflecting the demographics of the US. However, Asians comprised 55% of the foreign born IT workers. California had the highest percentage of foreign born IT workers. *California, New York, Illinois, and Virginia had more foreign born IT workers than native born IT workers!*[59] This is dangerous.

By 2005, an astounding 400,000 Indian nationals were working in Silicon Valley. And the numbers grew as India continued to get more H-1B visas than any other country. [240]

Offshoring is a Losing Proposition for US

Foreign nationals working in the US persuaded executives to convert powerful US corporations into multinationals offshoring jobs to foreign countries. The ploy was to claim US markets are "mature," and the growth markets are in Asia. [378] However, the truth is that US businesses in these countries often instead of selling to local markets, exported goods and services back to be sold in the US. [372] One American professional frustrated by bad experiences trying to sell in Asian markets commented, "...*good luck ever collecting the contractual amount.*" [110]

Offshoring makes it hard to get justice in a legal dispute. For example, a programmer in Bombay India attempted to sell software code stolen from a US company. When the thief was caught, an *FBI agent investigating the crime warned that US laws do not apply to foreign workers in foreign nations*. A conviction of the criminal was unlikely. Also, while China signed Trade-Related Aspects of Intellectual Property Rights (TRIPS) agreements, this did little to stop intellectual property theft. Piracy was still rampant. A legal agreement is useless if a culture and the courts in a foreign nation will not enforce the law. [133]

We Need an American Miracle Model

How do we protect our intellectual property when outsourcing? One tactic recommended to US companies was to *"make sure that the provider has substantial assets in the United States just in case."* [133] The smarter solution is to use a US company that only employs US citizens so US laws apply.

Our government R&D money needs to be more fairly distributed among states. And we need to stop funding R&D done by foreign students, foreign professors, and foreign countries.

Chapter 10

"Are We Losing Our Edge?"

Our Leaders were giving away our lead.

We have been the world leader in advanced commercial and military technology since WWII. For over 50 years our nation held *"unchallenged superiority in virtually every field of science and technology, from basic research to product development."* [553] So how were China, India and Korea *rapidly catching up*?

"Are We Losing Our Edge?" a 2006 *Time* magazine article said we needed to invest more. However, if we used a little common sense we'd stop and think. Our research spending skyrocketed, yet countries that had posed no threat, were now threatening us. Obviously, more spending is not the answer.

The article notes that the US with only 6% of the world's population, awarded the most PhDs in the world–over 40%. [553] What the article fails to say is that 50%+ of US high tech PhDs went to foreign students from *China, India, Korea and other countries.*

Our increased R&D spending was actually creating the threat. For example, the article said Edison Liu, who was born in Hong Kong and came to the US as a student, became clinical sciences director at our National Science Institute. Then in 2001 *the government of Singapore came knocking and offered Liu the directorship of its new Genome Institute.* His only consideration was the position and the money. He had no loyalty connection to the United States. He left. *Such defections from technology jobs in the US to foreign countries had become "disturbingly common."* [553]

American Brain Drain

Executives claimed that employing foreign workers is essential for the US to remain globally competitive. The exact opposite is true.

It will not be possible to be competitive when US corporations train our competition and deny Americans work experience in key technologies of the future. For example, globally the numbers of jobs in the computer industry were growing. Yet, *America's share of these jobs declined dramatically. Not because other nations independently developed competitive IT technologies, but because executives in American corporations transferred US technology and jobs offshore to foreign workers.*

Layoffs of Americans are costing our nation a tremendous brain drain. [29] Many of our top experts in the fields of computer software and telecommunications lost their jobs to foreign workers. *Ironically, the Americans who invented US technologies lost their jobs to foreign workers from countries where piracy of US technologies was rampant.*

A 2005 survey by *Electronic Engineering Times*, found Americans employed in high tech professions felt devalued and underpaid. Many said that outsourcing threatens the future of their profession in the US. *Only 10% thought our country would be able to maintain our technology leadership.* [452]

Americans have tremendous talent to invent. Their talent is being wasted. Of course, foreign workers in our labs will file some patents. However, this is overlooking what displaced Americans could have contributed. *What if some of the most important discoveries of our century are never made because we failed to protect American scientists and engineers?* Could they have invented a computer chip essential to our national defense, prevented an attack on our infrastructure, ended our dependence on foreign oil, found the cure for a worldwide pandemic ...?

It is Impossible to Out-Invent Theft

In some foreign cultures the theft of US intellectual property is accepted as common business practices. Some foreign competitors that cannot invent the technology see stealing our technology as a viable option. [166]

Both India and China have an unsavory history of piracy of US intellectual property. [121] For example, in 2000, it was reported that China's software piracy rate exceeded 90%! [380]

A 2003 *BusinessWeek* cover story, "The Rise of India," had the audacity to call Americans paranoid. It complained that India and China were unfairly being villianized. A commentary, "Meeting the Asian Challenge" criticized: *"Rather than embracing innovation, Americans seem to be concerned with adopting protectionist measures and trying to hold on to existing jobs. Rather than worrying about IT positions going offshore, the U.S. should focus on generating new jobs—in new industries—at home."* It claimed, *"there's no evidence of a major flight of educated jobs from the U.S."* [300] Of course, there is plenty of evidence.

Offshoring our IT jobs foolishly puts foreign workers in control of the security of our computer networks. Foreign espionage of US computer networks is rampant. Because of theft, from 1998 to 2000 US corporate spending on security increased 10 fold. American scientists may work years to invent a new technology that can be copied i.e. stolen from a computer file in a matter of seconds. American inventors cannot compete against foreign spies copying their work before they can apply for a patent. So, *we cannot accept IT "going offshore."*

Moreover, software has become integrated into high tech products [43] from communications devices, to household appliances, to cars, to missile guidance to airplane flight controls. It is dangerous for foreign programmers to take control of our programming. So again, *we cannot accept IT "going offshore."*

EXECUTIVES 'TRANSFERRING' US TECHNOLOGY

As US inventors create new designs that could keep the US globally competitive, instead executives offshore production to foreign countries. *It is impossible for our nation to be a technology leader when our new inventions are siphoned off as soon as they are created. American inventions should create jobs for Americans, not for foreign competition.*

Moreover, executives were dangerously shifting R&D offshore. For example, an *Electronic Design*'s 2005 Reader Profile Survey showed that *a disturbing new trend emerged: 52% reported their companies had begun outsourcing design work.* Electronics design jobs were being offshored to China and India. [615] And, 60% of those surveyed reported that their companies had outsourced manufacturing. This is noteworthy because close contact with manufacturing helps engineers get ideas for new designs. [615]

The More We Spend, The Greater the Threat?

We invested more in R&D than any other country. In 2000 alone, *we invested $265 billion on research* which exceeded the total combined spending by Japan, Germany, France and the UK. [170]

In 2006, in response to intense lobbying President Bush announced an American Competitiveness Initiative that would <u>double federal funding on basic research.</u> The money was to finance R&D in nanotechnology, alternate energy, and supercomputing. It would also give permanent R&D tax credits, and finance the training of 70,000 more high school teachers for science and math. [553]

In 2006, our government and businesses spent a combined $284 billion on research. ***<u>We funded 44% of the world's R&D</u>*** No other country even came close. [484] *So how is it possible with this level of investment, that our technology leadership is threatened by Asia?* Something is terribly wrong.

They Want More Taxpayer Money!

US executives who "transferred" our jobs to foreign workers try to defend their actions by claiming that the corporations are no longer US corporations. They claim they are multinational corporations that must compete in the global economy.

Yet, when these executives want our tax money to finance research they suddenly revert to being US corporations.

For example, Microsoft and Intel executives in 2002 warned that we were at risk of losing our technology leadership. They said we must spend more tax money on research because, *"government spending seeds university and corporate spending."* [226]

Did *Intel disclose to Congress that three years earlier it built a design center in India to work on* computer chip software *for* high end computers? Did it disclose that in August 2002 it announced plans to spend $200 million to build a design center in India where it would triple the number of engineers? Did Intel disclose that it had invested in almost 30 startups in India that would be competing against our businesses in strategic areas such as communications? [775]

Again in 2004, executives were pressuring Congress to invest more in R&D saying that the money was needed to keep the US competitive globally. *They wanted us to fund more university research. And, they wanted more tax breaks in the form of new tax credits for R&D spending, and accelerated depreciation write offs. They incredulously complained of inadequate US government R&D spending while lobbying against any limits on offshore hiring.* [114] [222]

What good is funding more research when the offshore "globalization" scheme enables foreign nations to quickly and easily steal our new technology? [81]

Americans Taxed to Fund Foreign Research!

In some situations programs which were supposed to help the US compete with foreign nations were incredulously doing the opposite.

By 1995, US government research labs had provided over $75 million in research money to companies from South Korea, to the former Soviet Union, to Germany, France and England. This does not include all the money or all the foreign governments receiving money from these programs. Moreover, our government has sold and given away valuable technologies created in US government labs to foreign nations. [172]

We were being taxed to pay an estimated <u>*44% of the entire R&D*</u> *done in all the Organization of Economic Co-operation and Development (OECD) countries. While at the same time these countries were encouraged to invest in basic research so that they could compete against us.* [523] It appears highly contradictory to sell joint collaboration with undeveloped nations as a strategy to benefit the US, and conversely as a competitive strategy to the countries we are helping. Why should we pay for creating our own competition?

Securing our Computers & Labs is Imperative

Americans worked and invested in our country filling up huge reservoirs of technology for our economy and defense. However, foreign nations are punching holes and draining us dry faster that we can refill. First, we must plug the holes in our security before we put in any more investments.

Next, we need to identify American talent and give them the tools and resources they need to invent new technologies to revive our economy, and bolster our national defense.

Chapter 11

Fake News & Suppressed

Stories

"If a nation expects to be ignorant and free, in a state of civilization, it expects what never was and never will be." –Thomas Jefferson

Where were the real news stories? Globalization has compromised our technology leadership, created horrific levels of US trade deficits, and jeopardized our national security. Yet, the economic attack on America has received alarmingly little coverage in our news media.

Foreign nations used American PR firms to develop a plethora of terms to promote offshoring to Asia such as:

- *Rise of Asia, Free Trade, New Economy, Nation of Immigrants, Globalization, World Class Workforce, Best and Brightest Workers, Global Markets, Emerging Markets, Global Community, Global workforce, Knowledge Transfer, Narrowing the Digital Divide, Moving up the Value Chain, Brain Drain, Brain Circulation, Diversity, Outsourcing Cost Savings, Genius Immigrant Entrepreneurs, Offshore R&D Cost Savings, Multiculturalism. ....*

And the negative PR terms used to belittle critics:

- *Protectionist, Fear, Hysteria, Racist, Xenophobic, Hegemon, Decline of America, American Market Mature, American Children not as smart ... ...*

Fake News Crafted by PR Companies

"Fake news" reports generated by major corporations and even our government were broadcasted by America television stations. In 2006, the FCC began to investigate and found these fake *news segments were crafted by public relations (PR) companies that had a lucrative business creating reports that mimicked real news.* [534]

The FCC was shocked at how pervasive fake news broadcasting had become. Major US corporations and 20 federal agencies were being investigated. The point of contention was the requirement that viewers must be advised about who produced video segments. The companies all claimed that they did proper disclosures and did not try to hide that these were promotional videos. However, when the fake news was broadcast, television stations failed to tell viewers who produced the videos.

Over 25,000 people wrote to the FCC to complain about the fake news segments. One outspoken critic said, *"Essentially it's corporate advertising or propaganda masquerading as news...The Public obviously expects their news reports are going to be based on real reporting and real information. If they are watching an advertisement for a company or a government policy, they need to be told."* [534]

Companies were also paying PR companies to write articles. The "news" was submitted to business and technical journals to be published under the name of a staff writer. This falsely represented the source of the information. These articles included fake quotes of conversations that never occurred, and glowing rhetoric praising entrepreneurs. So Americans were reading and making investment decisions based on fake news articles.

In 2010, our government spent $945 million on advertising contracts to tell people about entitlements, issue warnings, etc. Fifteen of Obama's Cabinet agencies had Twitter accounts. [1003]

Real News or Outsourcing Plugs?

"Globalization Gets Personal," a 2008 *NBC Nightly News* segment, *plugged personal outsourcing to India from tutoring our children, to legal work, to medical outsourcing, to tax preparation.* It even suggested checking out how outsourcing workers in India spend their off hours, and called Bangalore the *"Silicon Valley of the East."* [650]

"India the last Frontier ...Can India, like China, become the next silicon success story – the "last frontier" for semiconductor manufacturing?" was an *EETimes* cover story in March 2007. The cover photo was an elephant's face painted with electronic circuit diagrams. And, a callout box on the cover told readers: *"For full coverage of developments in India and China also see pages 13, 19, 20, 22, and 25."* Stories listed were: "India's Chip Policy may Yield $5B in Foreign Funds," "SemIndia Looks Beyond Silicon and Beyond India," "Fab Craze in China is not Playing Out as Planned," and "Stumbling Blocks Start with Costs" a story about how India companies are trying to sell electronic products under its own brands. [620]

- *CMP logo on cover claims:* "The industry newsweekly for the creators of technology."

- *CMP Worldwide Media Networks has over 80 publications in over 32 countries.* [466]

Who's doing our Nielsen's Ratings?

A Dutch company, VNU, owned the Nielsen's ratings, and sold marketing research. VNU's biggest customer was the US. [472] In 2006, a group of bidders: AlpInvest Partners, The Blackstone Group, the Carlyle Group, Hellman & Friedman, Kohlberg Kravis Roberts & Co., Permira and Thomas H. Lee Partners offered $8.87 billion to acquire VNU. [470] Why was the Carlyle Group, a US defense contractor, trying to buy US Nielsen's ratings?

Media Perceptions and Deceptions

"Offshore Outsourcing: Perceptions and Misperceptions," a 2005 *WideAngle* report quoted the CEO of Infosys, Nandan Nilekani: *"everything you can send down a wire is up for grabs."* The report claimed *if these jobs had not been offshored, technology innovations would have automated or otherwise eliminated the jobs anyway.* Why would we want to incur foreign trade debt for jobs that we could automate?

The report complained that in the 2004 election, *"outsourcing made a convenient scapegoat for politicians," and that the impact of outsourcing and offshoring on the US economy and job market was exaggerated.* It said the Bureau of Labor Statistics could only track 3% of the mass layoffs in America to offshore outsourcing. This was a very clever deception. <u>Most outsourcing was still done inside the US by foreign owned bodyshops and American outsourcing companies.</u> So, it fails to count the jobs taken by H-1B, L1 and other visa holders. And, it fails to count the offshore operations of American corporations that are not outsourced, but hire foreign workers. And, it fails to count the jobs lost under the cloak of acquisitions and mergers.

It said that Reuters announced in February 2004 that it would offshore six lower-level financial reporting journalist jobs to India. The first two months of the following year the number of stories on offshoring financial reporting doubled. Did the writers have conflicts of interest?

According to the story, *McKinsey Global Institute acknowledged that EU countries suffered losses from offshoring, but claimed the US experienced a net gain because displaced Americans were able to find new jobs.* The segment also acknowledged that the wages in Bangalore were rising rapidly. Many US companies that had offshored experienced significant hidden costs and were regrouping to have jobs returned to the US. [561]

"Why They Hate Us"

After the 9/11 attacks most Americans were outraged at this killing of innocent Americans. So *where did the story come from that we felt it was somehow our fault and were asking "why do they hate us?"*

The answer can be found in the October 2001 <u>*Newsweek cover story, "Why They Hate Us,"*</u> by <u>Fareed Zakaria. He was *given several awards for writing this article*</u>. [639] Who's is he? He's a Muslim born in India who came to the US as a foreign student. He got a B.A. from Yale and a Ph.D. from Harvard. Who paid for his expensive education? In 1999 Esquire Magazine named Zakaria, *"one of the 21 most important people of the 21ˢᵗ Century."* Zakaria also wrote articles in *The Washington Post, The New York Times, The Wall Street Journal, and The New Yorker.*

PBS gave Zakaria his own show in 2005: "Foreign Exchange with Fareed Zakaria." A 2007 story, "Sizing Up the Competition" promoted offshoring. He talked with Rajat Gupta about OECD, globalization, and huge market opportunities in Asia. [640] Did Zakaria have a conflict of interest not only because he was from India, but also because his brother Arshad became *"head of New Vernon Capital, <u>the largest hedge fund investing in India</u>."* [641] Recall *OECD used our taxes to fund 44% of R&D done in 'developing' countries.*

In 2007, Zakaria wrote an essay criticizing America for *"fear-based" policies on immigration, trade, and terrorism.* [641] In 2009, he wrote, "Learning to Live with Radical Islam."

Glenn Beck called Zakaria an *"America basher and useful idiot."* So, in March 2011 on the *Tonight Show Zakaria responded: "I'm an immigrant. I'm not an American by accident of birth, as Glenn Beck is. I'm American by choice. I came to this country."* He said Beck's criticizing him and Obama was "coded" racism. And, *"You've got a country that is increasingly a mixture of minorities."* [1011] *To get his student visa required signing a legal agreement that he would return to India when his studies were completed. When he 'chose' to stay did he break our immigration laws?*

Where was Media Coverage to Warn US?

"Not Enough Asian Faces on the Telly?" The Indus Entrepreneurs (TiE) complained American television needed more Asian faces for diversity. [592] Has the number of "Asian Faces" on US television increased while our nation has been at war? Does it reflect our demographics?

One Asian face that should have been on the "telly" more was Hemant Lakhani. He was convicted in 2005 for trying to sell shoulder-fired missiles to terrorists with the intent to kill Americans. Lakhani was *recorded negotiating to sell 50 missiles to shoot down US jetliners simultaneously in multiple US cities!* His demeanor on the tapes was described as gleeful. Yet his sinister plot and trial received scant US media coverage. Disturbingly, Lakhani had lived in Britain for *45 years* as a soft spoken women's apparel salesperson. Why would a British national who originated from India want to kill Americans? [216] [217] [218] Moreover, Lakhani did not work alone. Manthena "Vijay" Raja made a plea bargain and admitted in a US federal court hearing that he laundered $86,000 supplied by *a man living in the United States going by the name "Mr. Haji."* Two other defendants, Yehuda Abraham a jeweler in New York and Moinudden Ahmed Hameed also from India, pleaded guilty to transferring money to fund Lakhani's evil attack on America. [218] Who is Mr. Haji? Yet most Americans probably don't even know about this dangerous plot to kill Americans.

"The IndUS Entrepreneurs (TiE) to Open Dubai Chapter," is another story that should have gotten major critical news coverage. TiE a "non-profit global network" based in our Silicon Valley was helping to spawn IT and media technology startups in Dubai. While our economy was in a tailspin, naturalized US citizens Rajat Gupta and Kanwal Rekhi were speakers for TiE Dubai's 2003 inauguration.

Time to End Fake News

Fake news and news slanted to benefit foreign interests has harmed our nation. It is vital that our media not be foreign owned, nor should it be owned by immigrants using the media to benefit their country of origin. Our government needs to limit the scope of media control that can be exercised by a few individuals or a small number of entities.

We need people in control of our media who do not have conflicts of interest and that value and want to protect America and the American people. When a foreign nation is stealing US technology we need to know. When goods sold by a foreign nation or terrorists group are funding military and terrorists plots that threaten Americans we need to know.

Chapter 12

Our Terrible Trade Deficit with

China

Our Government Mismanaged Trade with China.

The biggest reported trade deficit we have is with China. The size of this deficit is actually even worse than it appears on the surface because it has been cloaked by China's buying US government treasury bonds instead our US goods and services.

It was a long running fabricated deception that China provided a big market opportunity for American made products. For example, in 1997 it was reported that *China only bought 1.7% of our exports, while in contrast we bought 33% of China's exports.* [173]

Despite continual warnings of the consequences of trade imbalances caused by offshoring to China our government failed to stop this dangerous trend. The trade deficit jumped to record levels year after year. By 2002, the deficit with China ran an alarming $103 billion. In 2003 the deficit hit another record at $124 billion. In 2004, it climbed to $162 billion. [179]

An article, "We Must End our Disastrous Trade Policy with China," in 2005, wrote that Congressman Sanders protested that for several years executives told Congress that there were huge market opportunities to sell our products in China. Yet instead of sales we had a horrific trade deficit. [428] By 2006, *our trade deficit with China far surpassed any deficit we ever had with any country.* [490] [179]

A Preposterous Situation

Out trade deficit with China is a preposterous situation. *How many US patents and copyrights have been infringed? How many US corporations fleeced?* For example, according to some estimates more than 90% of the software and DVDs in China are pirated. [427]

Executives moved the production of US goods to foreign countries. Ironically, our crushing deficit with China is almost exclusively from buying goods that were originally designed and produced in the US. China did not pay for the years of research, market development, infrastructure, and other investments that built these companies. Moreover, China is selling US products to countries that otherwise would have purchased these products from the US. Thus offshoring to China is also causing US trade deficits with other nations to grow. *We also hit record level deficits with Japan, Europe, OPEC, Canada, Mexico and more.* [490] [179]

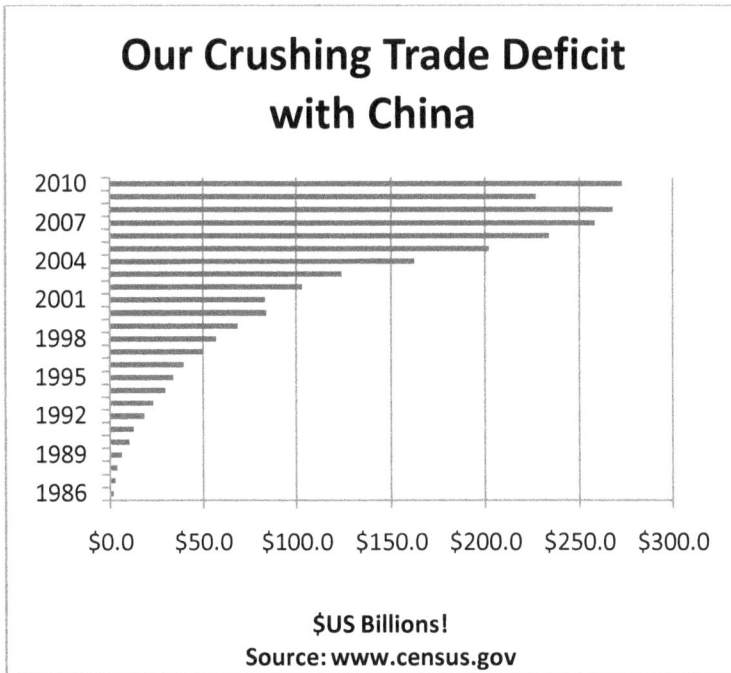

Our Crushing Trade Deficit with China

$US Billions!
Source: www.census.gov

Folly of Focusing on Currency

Some think the best way to address our trade imbalance is to reduce the real trade value of the dollar. [570] For example, in 2005 US manufacturers complained that the Chinese Yuan was undervalued by almost 40%! [179] However, Greenspan warned that a higher valued Yuan would increase the price of Chinese goods for Americans. [179]

The concept that the devaluing of the dollar will alleviate the US trade deficit is folly. We are in too deep for this to work. Even though China manipulated their currency for unfair trade advantage against us, devaluing the dollar at this point could prove unwise. This strategy fails to take into account that *executives in Corporate America dismantled US operations, closed US factories, laid off US workers, and "transferred" production to China. When this happened they eliminated the American source*. As a result many of the products and services needed by US citizens and US government are only produced in foreign countries, or the amount produced in the US is well below the demand to meet our nation's needs.

If we pressure China and other countries to revalue their currency when we are dependent on them for certain products and services, all we will accomplish is increasing the cost of our imports. For example, when the US dollar depreciated compared to the Japanese yen in 2002 and 2003 it did not decrease our trade deficit, *quite the opposite–our trade deficit got worse*. [430]

Devaluing the dollar may have helped two decades ago. However, now it may cause more harm than good. Foreign governments could buy even more US companies, US real estate, and other US assets taking unacceptable influence over our government and our country. What we need are strategic progressive tariffs to transition production back to our country.

China Threat to US Technology Leadership

"U.S. Could Lose the SciTech Edge to China, Experts Fear," a 2010 *Fox News* article reported that China had the *"world's fastest supercomputer,"* and may soon surpass us as the world's technology leader. The National Academy of Engineers (NAE) warned about *"our inability to keep up with China."* Charles M. Vest, president of the NAE said we *need to increase spending on education and R&D.* [987] _The hole in his argument – **in 2009, 2010, and 2011, we spent triple the amount of money that China did on R&D**_. [990] There was no way China should have been able to compete with us. In 2011 we spent $405.3 billon, with two thirds going for defense. If the world is so dangerous that we are forced to spend that much on defense, why in the world would we be continuing student visas, offshoring and outsourcing to foreign nations? _The more we spend, it appears the more danger we are facing._

China IT Planned to Grow 2,700%!

Gartner estimated that software exports from China would grow from *$850 million in 2001 to $27 billion by 2006.* Interestingly, 40% of these exports may be generated by Indian companies operating in China. [777]

China's Tariffs on US Goods!

Our average tariff on Chinese goods was just 2%, while China exacted a stiff 35% average tariff on American imports. _China imposed a 17% tax on chips imported for sale in China, and rewarded local production in China with a 14% rebate_ according to a 2004 complaint filed by our government. China was accused of violating WTO regulations. In response to US protests, a Chinese official defiantly said that Beijing would keep preferential policies favoring chips produced in China for "years to come." [168] The only reason China is a major chip buyer is because US corporations offshored production of our computers and electronics.

China Targeted Our Semiconductor Industry

That bears repeating– *The only reason China is a major chip buyer is because US corporations offshored production of our computers and electronics.* While our government failed to protect this industry vital to our economy and our national security, the Chinese government formed a Ministry of Information Industry that invested billions to position China to compete globally in the semiconductor industry.

In 2003, China produced over 12 billion semiconductors. By 2004, about 20% of the semiconductors bought in China were produced in China. China provided a short term cheap production processing service to enable it to take control of a strategic US industry. [168]

A Pentagon report warned in 2005, that the offshoring of US semiconductor manufacturing to Asia endangered the "*security and integrity of classified and sensitive circuit design information.*" [165] The 33-nation Wassenaar agreement restricting the export of sensitive chip manufacturing equipment had failed. High risk nations were not supposed to have access to our leading edge fabrication equipment, nor were they to have access to sensitive technology secrets. And, countries we viewed as partners also jeopardized our national security. For example, the report claimed that Taiwan helped China's chip industry. [165]

US companies even offshored production of parts used in our weapons. For example, in June 2011, *The Washington Times* report, "Senators want China to Assist Probe of counterfeit Weapons Parts," said that China was refusing to help investigate. These *electronic counterfeit parts were found in our high tech weapons* systems. The US had a ban on Chinese bidding on supplying our weapons programs. However, there was a waiver for buying from China if the parts were no longer produced in the US and the only source was to buy from Chinese companies. [989]

We Fed the Tiger

"Who Fed the Tiger?" Pat Buchanan wrote in 2010: *"For decades, corporate America championed investing in China and trade with China, though <u>the massive transfer of U.S. factories, technologies and jobs was clearly empowering China and weakening America.</u>"* [959]

In turn, a US government commission found that *"China is adopting a highly discriminatory policy of favoring domestic producers over foreign manufacturers...<u>the government of China appears determined to exclude foreigners from bidding on government contracts</u> ..."* China is pursuing *"economic nationalism."* Buchanan concluded, *"The day of the globalist has come and gone."* [959]

Globalization was a ploy used by Asia to lure what some call "useful idiots" into betraying our nation for a few years of multimillion dollar bonuses. If the US falls, the tiger will have these "useful idiots" for a tasty second course.

We need new leaders who will end our trade deficit with China.

Chapter 13

China Armed and Dangerous

Corrupt US Leaders Armed Communist China.

A 2002 article, "China is a Threat to America," on *NewsMax.com* challenged claims by our media, professors, and politicians that China is a "strategic partner." It argued that China exported missile and nuclear warfare equipment to countries in the Middle East including Iran and Iraq. And, said *our leaders are dangerously ignoring "years of espionage and covert political influence through contributions to US political campaigns."* [577]

The promoters of "globalization" never told us that buying goods "Made in China" was funding a massive military buildup that posed a threat to our country and our children's future. The bulk of the money went to the Communist Chinese government, not the Chinese people who were paid wages like 30 cents an hour, or were exploited as slave labor and paid nothing.

By 1997, our $105 billion trade deficit with China enabled the Chinese government to buy submarines, airplanes, missiles, and more from Russia and other countries. [173]

The Bush-Clinton-Bush presidencies let China amass $360 billion in foreign reserves according to an article written by Pat Buchanan in 2003. China used this money to purchase 450 missiles aimed at Taiwan, and fund the development of longer-range *missiles capable of attacking U.S. bases in the region.* [231]

Our Government Endangered Americans

"Red Tide: The Chinese Communist Targeting of America," a 1997 report faulted our government for turning China into a dangerous military threat. *The report alleged that several former US government officials may have committed high treason when they were recruited to lobby for China.* According to this report our government allowed the Chinese military through its People's Liberation Army (PLA) to incorporate *thousands of front companies* in the United States that, "*enable China's military to infiltrate hundreds of thousands of intelligence agents into every nook and cranny of America and the West – into businesses, universities, research centers, high tech laboratories, into the U.S. government itself, where they are stealing hundreds of thousands of high tech (civilian and military) secrets.*" [173]

The report protested the "*treasonous patent giveaway*" which provided China with an electronic copy of 160 years of US patent disclosures. [173] The report also claimed that our government sold China old US defense factories at auction and US technology at cut rate prices that enabled China to build stealth aircraft. And, it quoted the Vice Commander Lt. General Mi Zhenyu from the Academy of Military Sciences in Beijing, "*for a relatively long time it will be absolutely necessary that we quietly nurse our sense of vengence...We must conceal our abilities and bide our time.*" [173] What a sinister threat.

OTHER REPORTS ALSO BLAMED OUR GOVERNMENT FOR ARMING CHINA

"Clinton-Approved Computer Exports Help China Build Atomic Bombs," a 2002 article claimed that Sun Microsystems along with other US computer companies persuaded the Clinton administration to allow the sale of high-speed computers to China. This dangerous export policy received a "scathing report" in 1999 from the General Accounting Office. *These advanced US computers enabled the Chinese army to design lightweight nuclear weapons capable of precision atomic attacks against the US.* [278]

"Q: Has Clinton's China policy put U.S. National Security at Risk?" a 2003 report said our government *"armed a new enemy."* The article claimed that prior to Clinton's presidency (1993-2001), <u>US technologies were so highly advanced over China's that China did not pose a military threat. However, by the end of Clinton's presidency China was armed with advanced military technology obtained from the United States.</u> [279]

Our government also endangered our nation when it shared technology secrets with "partners." For example, in 2006, prosecutors in Taiwan indicted United Microelectronics (UMC) executives Robert Tsao and John Hsuan for investing in Hejian Technology Corp, a Chinese chip fabricator without obtaining Taiwan government approval. The investigation found that Tsao made this investment knowing that Hejian was infringing on close to 200 UMC patents. Tsao said that his client <u>would only buy chips produced in China.</u> [448] What happened to *"free trade?"*

Questioning China's Military Build Up

China has built missiles, warships, and planes, and "nuclear, biological and chemical weapons." [199]

Defense Secretary Donald H. Rumsfeld questioned China's military buildup in 2005. He did not know of any country that was a threat to China. To downplay the very real threat to America, a Chinese official commented: *"Do you truly believe that the U.S. is threatened by the emergence of China?"* [609]

Two years later Vice President Dick Cheney also criticized China's military buildup and said it was, *"not consistent with China's stated goal of a peaceful rise."* [608]

"Pentagon Sounds Alarm at China's Military Buildup," was a 2010 *Wall Street Journal* story. It said Congress was warned that China was advancing its electronic warfare capabilities, expanding its missile range, and appeared to be the source of cyber attacks stealing our military secrets. [986]

Cyber Attacks Against US Businesses

"Google Not Only Target of China Hackers," a 2010 cbsnews.com report claimed: "*Chinese cyber-spies target dozens of U.S. companies, experts say, stealing valuable trade secrets.*" Peter Navarro, who wrote "The Coming China Wars," said "*It is a story about industrial espionage, coming from China, attacking American business and our economy. ...When they hack American business enterprises, it is a covert act of war on our economy at a time when their economy is growing at over 10 percent and we have a 10 percent unemployment rate.*" [958]

Thanks to "diversity" propaganda and H-1B visas China has insiders who can steal US corporate secrets. In contrast China tightly controls access to its computer networks. [958]

Internet access enables hackers in China to attack our computers. *It is estimated that China launches thousands of cyber attacks everyday to break into American computers.* For example, hackers in China broke into US Defense Department computers to steal aviation specs and software according to a 2005 news report. [475]

"Internet Traffic from U.S. Government Websites Was Redirected Via Chinese Servers," was a 2010 Fox News report. It said a Chinese government owned telecom firm "hijacked" internet traffic for 18 minutes. Hijack *victims were our Pentagon, Senate, and other government websites, along with high tech companies including IBM and Microsoft.* The U.S.–China Economic and Security Review Commission said they did not know if this was deliberate, nor did they know what was done with or to the data. However, they noted China has a history of "*malicious computer activities.*" Chris Smoak, a Georgia Tech research scientist, said that incidents like this occur with data channeled to foreign nations "*two or three times a year.*" He said internet data routing is susceptible to manipulation because, "*It's all based on trust.*" [879]

We Need to Secure Our Computers

Thanks to offshoring, China had the money to buy leading edge *computer networks that surpass the legacy systems used in much of the US government and business.* Because of outsourcing and offshoring, we could not afford to buy the latest computer network technologies we invented. [164]

Spies in our country legally and illegally need to be identified and prosecuted. We need new leaders in our government that are not compromised by investments in foreign nations.

Because our government deployed Internet technology hackers in foreign countries can attack computers in the United States. They do not even have to be in our country. *Highly sensitive data should not be put on computers connected to the Internet.* We need to limit and screen foreign internet access to US computer networks.

Chapter 14

India's Betrayal After Decades

of US Aid

Then: We provided aid to help India

Now: India poses an economic and military threat.

Prior to the 1950's we had little interaction with India. Then in 1951, we rushed 2 million tons of wheat to India to avert a famine. Next, we helped India improve its food production and store millions of tons of food. We continued providing US aid, generously responding to requests from the Indian government.

We gave billions of dollars of aid to India. Our taxes helped to construct 20 power plants in India intended to stimulate business and economic development. We also provided loan guarantees to help India obtain financing to stimulate private industry.

Most valuable of all, we provided extensive educational assistance to India. We helped fund building regional education colleges and agricultural universities. We provided India over 4,000 American advisors and consultants. *US Aid helped build the Indian Institute of Technology (IIT) in Kanpur and Kharagpur, and 14 regional engineering colleges.* (Narayana Murthy, founder of India's Infosys outsourcing firm, got his master's degree from IIT Kanpur in 1969.) US Aid also paid for students from India to travel to the United States and study in our universities. [352]

India Politics "Culture of Corruption"

Our aid was channeled through the India government which according to multiple sources is fraught with corruption.

- "*Politics, Crime Go Hand-in Hand in India,*" *a 2006 AP article claimed that a "rogues gallery of bandits, racketeers and murderers have filled the halls of power." And that an "endemic culture of graft" ran deep as a result of caste, religion, and distribution of wealth.* [595]

- "*Corruption 'Threatens India's Economic Growth,'* a 2011 BBC News report, said the "culture of corruption" in India's government and industry had grown from petty bribes into multi-billion dollar scandals that "point to a pervasive culture of corruption."* [926]

- "*The Financial Times: Corruption Besets India,*" a 2012 report said: "Corruption scandals have sullied India's reputation over the past 18 months." Corruption cost hundreds of billions.* [998]

- *The Financial Times reported in 2002 that 20% of the lower house of parliament in India had criminal backgrounds.* [90]

- "*Most bureaucracies are bloated, corrupt, and dysfunctional,*" a 2003 BusinessWeek story "The Rise of India" said India's lethargic legal system can take 20 years to resolve contract disputes.* [300]

"Castocracy" in America?

India claims to be the *"world's largest democracy."* However, Dr. G. Singh said that India was really a *"castocracy."* In 1997 he wrote an article, "The Post-1947 Brahmanist Order and its Ideological Foundation," that said Brahman hegemons control about 95% of the high level decision-making and management positions. And, *he claimed their stranglehold on management control is all encompassing from government, to business, to media, to universities, to police, to investment opportunities, and more.* [391] Are India's diaspora in our country using "*castocracy*" tactics in our government, businesses, media and universities to benefit their network to the detriment of other Americans?

Conspiracy or Coincidence?

India had a mere 6,800 programmers in 1985. [335] Is it miraculous coincidence that India happened to have tens of thousands of programmers ready for "export" to the United States just when the "Desperate Shortage of IT Workers" was brought to the attention of the US Congress five years later in 1990?

It does not make any sense that a country with India's economic problems would spend money to educate such massive numbers of programmers when it did not have jobs for them. It is not likely that any nation would make this much of an investment if they did not have a plan.

OOPS — THE TRUTH CAME OUT

America never had a high tech worker shortage–it was all a fraud. Every United States Congress member should read the 2005 article, "India's Story of Success: Promoting the Information Technology Industry," by Sarala V. Nagala online at *stanford.edu*. Her definition: *"Outsourcing and offshoring are synonyms that refer to the substitution of foreign (i.e. Indian) for domestic labor (i.e. American)."* [617]

India's unprecedented achievements were "not merely coincidental," Nagala said. [617] *She revealed that India's government pursued our IT industry because of its strategic importance economically, and in information warfare (IW).* According to Nagala, the government of India established a Ministry of Information Technology and plotted to become an IT Super Power controlling military and civilian communications networks globally.

She described how India's government exploited *"connections with the successful Indian diaspora"* in our country, and used financial incentives to sell outsourcing to Corporate America.

It was all carefully played like a game of chess.

India's diaspora were expected to seek executive positions in Corporate America, and then to "encourage" outsourcing our jobs to India. Nagala gave Vinod Khosla as an example when Sun Microsystems' offshored jobs to India. She wrote: *"the main source of India's budding prosperity is the outsourcing of jobs in information technology from the United States to India."* [617]

Our corporations were lured to offshore, she explained, because an IT worker in India cost only $8,000 per year compared to $78,000 for an American. Note that this had nothing to do with any high tech American worker shortages.

Diaspora in America gave financial "gifts" to Indian Institutes of Technology (IITs) because: *"Investing in the IITs can alleviate the problems caused by the shortage of computer professionals that has been predicted for the next several years."* [617] Guess who did the predicting.

Nagala connected the dots exposing that *TiE and other organizations formed by India's diaspora in the United States networked closely with the India government and to "those of their own origin."* [617]

She told how the India government was using the UN program "The Transfer of Knowhow Through Expatriate Nationals." Under this program the India's diaspora in the US are expected to make trips to India to disperse knowledge. [617]

While India and China ply the US with "global community," and "diversity" propaganda, only our leaders have been gullible enough to buy into this propaganda. Both these nations pursue nationalistic goals, and ethnic (racially exclusive) roles. Nagala wrote that underneath the surface these two nations were *"rank with competition and secrecy."* [617]

Nagala's assertions are confirmed by multiple other sources as you will see.

India Diaspora Strategically Dispersed Globally

India's government keeps close ties with nonresident Indians (NRIs) positioned in the United States and approximately 120 other countries. They were strategically placed–like in chess.

While the majority of people in India are Hindus, it also has more than 10% or about 100 million Muslims. This may help explain why in the 1970's and 1980's many people from India moved to work in the Middle East. They and their children born in the Middle East were *not granted citizenship because they were not Arabs.* By 2005, India had:

- *1.5 million people in Saudi Arabia*
- *1.2 million (half the population) in the United Arab Emirates*
- *500,000 in Kuwait*
- *175,000 in Qatar*
- *1,800 in Syria*
- *800 in Iran*
- *500 in Afghanistan*
- *110 in Iraq, etc.*
- *Interestingly they also had 45,300 in Israel.* [618]

Did our Congress know about the India Diaspora in the Middle East and other countries when it approved the H-1B visa program in 1990? What if this close knit network channels US military and national security secrets to its members in the Middle East?

By 2007, India Diaspora had grown to 2.5 million in the United States, 6.4 million in Europe, 2.8 million in Africa, 50,500 in Hong Kong, 13,400 in Japan, and 16,044 in Russia. Interestingly, India had only 305 in China. [618] Why are the two countries leery of opening their doors to each other?

India increased the enrollment of people from India in MBA programs in the US and other countries around the world. [240] Management 'consulting' jobs were key to selling offshoring.

India's Nuclear Test Deception

Despite all our aid, and getting billions from US offshoring, in 1995, our satellites captured photos of a nuclear test site in India. The photos were shown to India in an effort to deter nuclear testing. Our officials naively thought India would not risk the Clinton administration's policy of promoting outsourcing that was a boon to India's economy. They were wrong.

Our CIA was <u>not able to recruit even one spy</u> to keep informed on India's nuclear program, nor was the CIA able to eavesdrop on Indian leaders. [252] No diversity! Yet, India may have tens of thousands of spies in the US. India assured the American Embassy on March 26, 1998, that it had no plans to test for three to six months. However, *"<u>The Indians' denials were part of a sophisticated disinformation campaign.</u>"* [139]

Two months later, *May 25, 1998, India exploded a nuclear bomb catching the US totally off guard <u>fooling our State Department, our CIA, our Pentagon, and our National Security Council</u>. Commenting on how the US was blindsided one US official asked, "Did we help them go to school in some way?"* [139] The answer is– yes we did. [252]

In response, Clinton imposed economic sanctions. However, he made the sanctions a joke when a couple of months later he signed the *1998 H-1B bill* that increased the annual cap from 65,000 to 90,000 visas. An Indian computer science PhD student studying in the US said:

> *"Just about every Indian working here sees the hypocrisy. When America condemns India's nuclear tests, but <u>it lets Indians come into this country and make U.S. dollars to send back home</u>. Were the U.S. government to decide to lock us out because of the tests, the current Indian government would be out of power within a week and there would be no more testing."* [213]

What did India care if the US withheld $140 million in aid, and opposed a $1.5 billion World Bank loan. H-1B money transfers that diaspora sent back home to India were in the billions.

India Planted Diaspora to Drive Offshoring

Just months after India's nuclear test deception, in November 1998, *businessweek.com*'s cover story, "India's WHIZ KIDS, Inside the Indian Institutes of Technology's Star Factory," praised how India "exported" IIT graduates to US graduate schools. India expected these students to follow the example of Taiwan, and seek *executive positions in America Corporations, so that they could then channel US jobs and technology to India*. [303]

"Whiz Kids?" "Star Factory?" This isn't news. It's PR.

India Government Recruited US Diaspora

A *welcome-nri.com* website claimed to be *"the Most Comprehensive Information Resource of Non-Resident Indians"* (NRIs). A report in 2000, "Govt Sets Up NRI Group on IT", said India recruited a *"select group of nonresident infotech professionals from Silicon Valley of the United States."* [368] India's government handpicked NRIs were:

■ *"Kanwal Rekhi, president of the TiE group, Vinod Khosla of the US firm KPCB, Suhas Patil of Cirrus Logic, K.B. Chandrasekhar chairman of Exodus Corp. USA, and Sabeer Bhatia of hotmail.com fame."* [368] *(See also Rekhi and Khosla big fundraisers for Obama in Democracy Hijacked book)*

These NRIs were to report to India's Minister of IT who would arrange meetings. And, they were to work with India's Director Ministry of IT, and India's Secretary in the Ministry of IT. These NRIs were *"expected to keep the (India) government abreast of the latest developments taking place in the infotech world and also the market trends."* [368]

Specifically these diaspora were to promote offshoring our IT jobs to India, to help educate IT workers in India to fill offshored jobs, and to help IT incubators in India obtain US venture capital. Ultimately the objective was to empower India so that it could achieve its targeted global goals.

"Changing the Face of American Business"

"*The Indians are Coming—How Management Thinkers from India are Changing the Face of American Business*," a 2005 article provided insight into their too subtle goal of "*changing the face of American business.*" They assert, "*While no one can predict the Indian thinkers' long term impact on American businesses.*" [240] However, their impact is quite apparent. All their talk about the "Rise of India," and the US receding and losing our technology leadership shows that they knew exactly what they were doing. (See also the book Democracy Hijacked to learn about "Obama's Team India." Especially note Obama's *Chief Information Officer* appointment.)

Planned Technology Transfer

"*NASSCOM's survey during 1999-2000 indicates a reversal in the mode of services offered by India. In 1991-92, offshore services accounted 5% and on-site services 95% of the total exports. However, during 1999-2000 offshore services contributed over 40 percent of the total exports.*" [161] India was providing financial incentives for American corporations to offshore to India according to *indiaembassey.org.* [161]

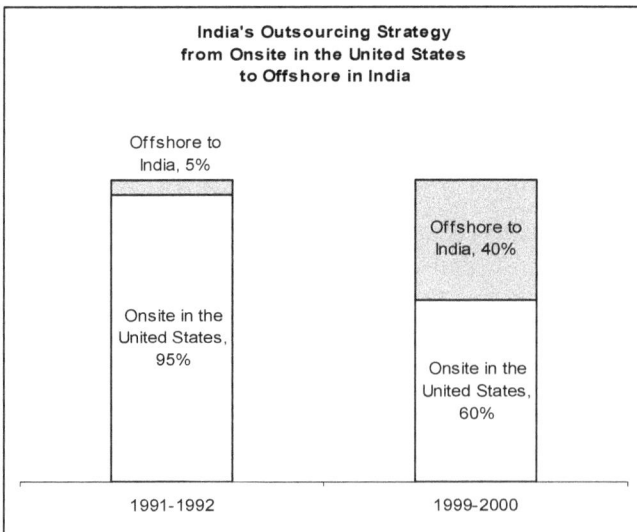

India's Outsourcing Strategy
from Onsite in the United States
to Offshore in India

Offshore to India, 5%

Offshore to India, 40%

Onsite in the United States, 95%

Onsite in the United States, 60%

1991-1992   1999-2000

Planned Takeover of Our Telecom Industry

In 2000, Chidandand Rajghatta wrote in the *Indian-Express.com*: "*IIT alumni Arun Netrtravalli took over as President of the legendary Bell Labs, <u>the fount of 30,000 inventions</u>.*" [330] This sounds suspiciously like someone is planning to take a drink.

"<u>*Wireless Whisper: Desi Network Begins to Take over Telecom World*</u>" was the disturbing title of an *indiaexpress.com* article in 2000. (Desi is a slang term for people from India) The "Desi" network penetrated the executive ranks of *US telecom companies* such as: *AT&T, Bell, Lucent, Cisco and Qualcomm.* Next, they *founded several telecom startups companies* which: "*In at least half a dozen cases, the Indians founders have sold their companies to giant conglomerates for fortunes in excess of $500 million.*" [244] Did they have people on both sides negotiating these deals i.e. *were diaspora from India in the executive ranks of the American corporations buying Indian founded startups?*

They argued that we should stop objecting to the transfer of US technology to India because there were so many people from India embedded in the US technology sector. And, it claimed that *the government of India organized a group of people from India living in the US to lobby the US Congress for its benefit.* [244]

Protecting communications is vital to our security. Yet a 2004 CBS News story, "Out of India," stated that: "*There are few aspects of your telephonic life that do not sooner or later end up in India.*" And that India services "*all parts of the world.*" [308]

Members of Congress should read the revealing September 7, 2002, article, "Tech Start-ups: Indus Valley Circa 2002" by Shymanuja Das. The article claimed India was sending a "*message to the world*" that it planned to take control of the telecom industry. India planned to make sure "*that when the networks of tomorrow run, they will be controlled by Indian brainpower.*" Their ultimate goal: "*An India that would be home to all the intelligence that would flow in the nerves of global networks.*" [378]

US Defense R&D!

"*Indian immigrants in America account for less than 0.75% of the US population,*" yet they got "*more than 20 times*" *that amount* of our *Department of Defense R&D jobs,* according to a 2007 article, "Skilled Indian Immigrants Create Wealth for America," on INDOLink.com,–"*Linking Indians Worldwide*." [685]   *It said university professors selected "younger post-doctoral fellows and graduate students, also of Indian origin, for their research efforts." The research "ranged from homeland security to missile technology, advanced ceramics and munitions ..."* The stated goal was to "*maintain America's superiority in military technology.*" [685]

Does anyone believe it is India's goal to help us maintain our military superiority? Foreigners should not be given access, much less be doing this research.

India's Military Buildup

Bush signed an agreement to "share" US civilian nuclear technology and to supply India with nuclear fuel in July 2005. He did this despite India's nuclear test deception history, refusal to sign a nuclear non-proliferation agreement, and refusal to pressure Iran to stop its efforts to develop an atomic bomb. [500]

"Building a Modern Arsenal in India," a 2007 article reported India was planning to spend $40 billion on buying weapons, jet fighters, tanks and submarines. India has a history of buying weapons from Russia, so US companies were competing for this business. [658]

By 2012 *India surpassed China as the largest arms buyer in the world*. India bought most of its weapons from Russia–its cold war ally. Russia was the world leader in selling weapons; the *United States ranked second in weapons sales*. [1002] So US offshoring to India funds buying weapons from Russia. Should we be selling weapons around the world?

Planned Takeover Over of Our IT Industry

Immigrants from India played lead roles in forming dotcom companies. Just like demolition experts analyze a structure and strategically place their blasting devices at supports, the dotcom demolition crash was used to flatten our IT job market structure and pave the way for offshoring IT and other high tech jobs. India *lured US corporations reeling from losses and tight budgets into offshoring R&D to "save money."* They lured US banks and US venture capital investors financing offshoring and startups. To attract investors they claimed the growth markets were in Asia.

Balance of Power

India was *in the top 10 list of countries that received US aid*. Despite all our aid, we were unable to count on India for support at the United Nations. A 1999 analysis by *heritage.org* evaluating UN voting by countries that received US aid reported that India was at the top of the list of countries *voting against us 81% of the time*, China was number 6 voting against us 73% of the time. [353]

Recall the 2008, *Electronic Engineering Times* article "India Rides Growth Wave into New Age of Tech Globalization," reported India was *"forging IT partnerships with neighbors ... China, Egypt, Pakistan, Australia, Dubai..."* India was forming an axis intended to takeover global IT and technology industries. The article said, "*its arrival marks a turning point in the shift of Industry's balance of power from West to East*." [673] This was no coincidence. It was craftily planned. They were positioning for checkmate.

Chapter 15

India Targets America's

Economic Core

There is an old Indian story where a worker only asks for a single grain of rice for his payment– and that the payment double each payday. The king was embarrassed the first payday to give the worker a meager single grain of rice. The next payment two grains of rice did not seem enough. Payments continued: 4 grains of rice, 8 grains of rice, 16 grains of rice, 32 grains of rice, 64 grains of rice, 128 grains of rice, 256 grains, 512 grains of rice ... the payments soon grew out of control. The payments began bankrupting the kingdom. The king finally realized that he had been deceived by the illusion of a humble payment.

In the same way outsourcing to India started out with the representation that the payments were humble amounts. But, just like in the story there was deception. Outsourcing is bankrupting our nation and destroying our economy.

An article on *corpwatch.org* wrote: "*Some experts say the growth in offshore tech services is less about increased U.S. demand than about aggressive marketing by India firms. Some of the biggest are Infosys, Wipro Technologies and Tata Consulting Services (TCS), all based in India.*" [105] Also, *umsl.edu* found that the 2002 dramatic increase in tech design offshoring was driven by aggressive marketing by India's outsourcing companies like *Wipro, Infosys, and Tata*. [772]

"Rise of India"

"The Rise of India," a disturbing cover story in the December 8, 2003 issue of *BusinessWeek* reported: *"Quietly but with breathtaking speed, India and its millions of world-class engineering, business, and medical graduates are becoming enmeshed in America's new Economy in ways most of us barely imagines."* It said, *"India is accelerating a sweeping reengineering of Corporate America. Companies are shifting bill payment, human resources, and other functions to new, paperless centers in India."* [300]

It declared: *"India is penetrating America's economic core."* And that, China's offshoring impact was dwarfed compared to India's. China went after manufacturing which makes up 14% of our economy and 11% of US jobs. In contrast, *India targeted service industries that accounted for 60% of our economy and 66% of US jobs.* [300]

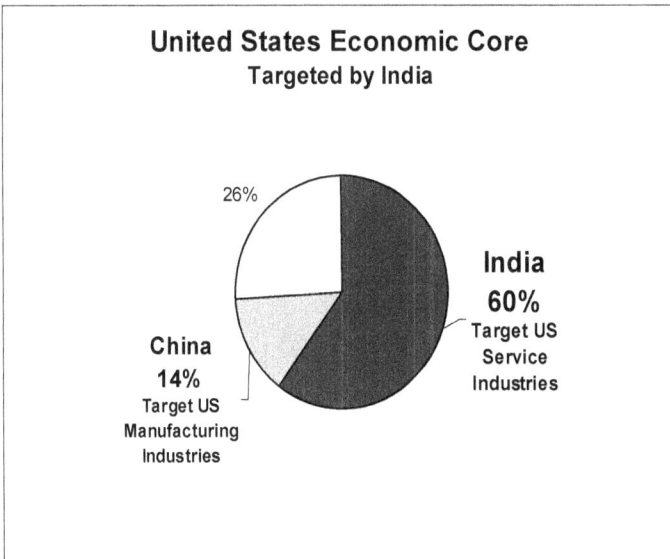

United States Economic Core
Targeted by India

26%

India
60%
Target US
Service
Industries

China
14%
Target US
Manufacturing
Industries

A McKinsey & Co./NASSCOM 'study' predicted that India's IT and BPO would skyrocket from about _$1 billion in 2000 to $24 billion by the year 2008_. That's a *2400% increase!* In 2008 alone, A.T. Kearney Inc. *forecasted 500,000 American financial services jobs would be offshored.* [300]

Predatory pricing was India's strategy. *"Corporate America is beating a path to India,"* because for the cost of one US programmer they could hire eight in India. This job "transfer" is *"wonderful for India"* but *"terrifying for many Americans."* The 2003 article said India had already taken jobs in *software, IT consulting, call centers* and *chip design.* [300]

- *Call center support was a $100 billion industry. GE had 12,000 employees in India "answering calls about consumer credit cards, giving IT technical assistance, and handling network security."* [6]

- *In 2003, there was a giant jump in offshore outsourcing.* [307] *The Meta group estimated that by 2008, 40% of American technical jobs will move offshore.* [107] [141] [73]

- *At a 2003 seminar in Mumbai, a Gartner research director said going offshore usually "means going to India." An analyst for Gartner heralded, "The pipeline is growing now."* [112]

India's next big targets were *our R&D jobs, financial analysis jobs, engineering jobs, and drug research jobs, and more. And, to add a point of humor, India wanted to sell US companies risk analysis services.* It also revealed that: *"India is even getting hard-wired into Silicon Valley."* [300]

India was persuading US companies to setup R&D in India. For example, India convinced Texas Instruments to build a microprocessor research center in Bangalore. India's *diaspora in Silicon Valley were raising billions in venture capital for software and chip startups. They required R&D be done in India for American startups to get venture capital.* In 2003, a shocking 33% to 75% of venture capital funded new startups in the United States had offshore R&D work done in India. [300]

And, our banks were also funding startups in India. Ash Lilani, born in India, became a senior VP of the Silicon Valley Bank. He took 20 Silicon Valley venture capitalists on a R&D scouting trip to India in 2003. *The bank planned to more than double its venture capital invested in R&D in India by 2005.* [300]

Planned Takeover of Our IT Industry

Historically, none of the major software products were invented in India. The truth is that India was notorious for piracy of US software. For example, in 1993, the software piracy rate in India was 89%. [182] Nonetheless, India's National Association of Software and Services Companies (NASSCOM) promoted India as the place to go for software development and services. [228]

By 1999, Indians took almost a third of the programming jobs in the US, and one fourth globally. [213] There is something very wrong when a group that is less than 1% of our population takes control of the strategic IT industry we created. India's IT industry was planning *a jump from about $3 billion in 1998 to $90 billion by 2008.* [124] As you can see this 30 fold *increase* was all part of a very calculated plan.

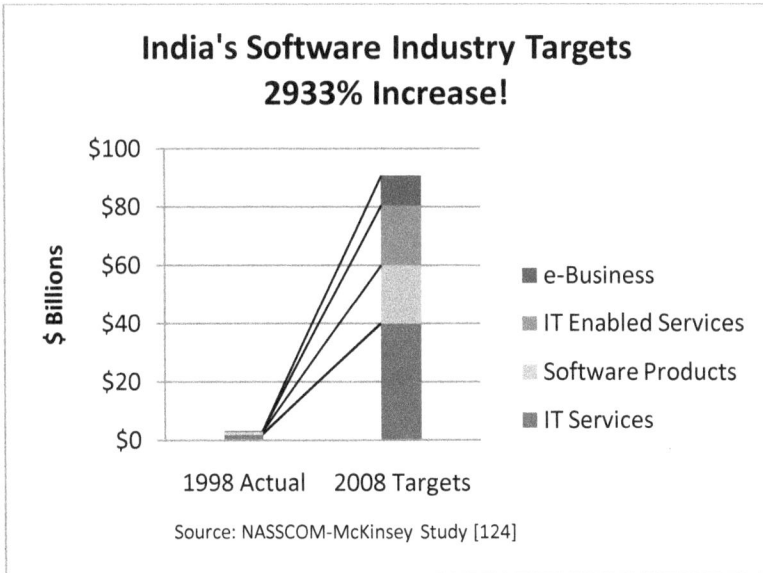

India's Software Industry Targets
2933% Increase!

Source: NASSCOM-McKinsey Study [124]

To facilitate the takeover of our IT industry, India's new ministry of IT in 2005 was helping IT entrepreneurs in India start businesses. [161]

India Targets Our BPO Jobs

In 2000, India claimed that the *"arrival" of the Internet opened up the global markets for India to provide service jobs for data mining, medical records, image processing, and technical documentation.* [334]

NASSCOM's President Mehta planned to travel to the US in 2001 to drum up more outsourcing business for India. [85] India's tactics ranged from insulting American workers, to claiming that offshoring benefited our economy. For example:

- *"Lack of Talent, Low Cost Make Outsourcing Inevitable for US," a 2003 indiaexpress.com article reported the president of NASSCOM claimed US companies find talent in India because talent is scarce in the US.* [307]

- *"India: IT Outsourcing Aids U.S. Other Economies", a 2003 asia.cnent.com story reported NASSCOM claimed that US banks, financial services companies, and insurance companies saved $6-$8 billion outsourcing IT to India.* [67]

- *"India's Tech Industry Defends H-1B, Outsource Roles," a 2003 ElectonicEngineeringTimes.com article reported McKinsey & Co.'s forecasted using foreign workers from India would net savings of $390 billion because having Americans do the work would have cost $532 billion.* [123]

However, there were hidden costs not included in their calculations. See the *Economic Circulation Model* in the book <u>False Prophets of False Profits</u>. Moreover, in 2002, *buyusa.gov* reported that ***"India continues to have high piracy rates for all types of copyrighted works.* "**[176]

- *Consider that by 2000 over 33% of our Fortune 500 companies had outsourced computer jobs to India. India in turn then exported software to 95 countries.* [161] *Then in 2004, India planned to "start developing technologies of its own." *[301]* Which logically means India had been exporting US technology to 94 foreign nations!*

Stock Investment Advice from India

JP Morgan Chase hired stock analysts in India. It does not take a genius to guess which stocks they will recommend to US investors. Of course, they will recommend companies in India and companies that offshore to India. And, if it follows the secretive nature of other offshore activities, *Americans will not even know the stock advice is coming from an analyst in India who may be more interested in taking more American jobs than helping Americans invest wisely.*

Wolf in Sheep's Clothing

In some cases American corporate clients may have been misled to believe that outsourcing work was being done in America by Americans. How? Infosys' *"raided major consulting companies"* such as IBM and Accenture hiring away their American management consultants to meet with clients and close deals. Infosys would then "hand off" the software development to programmers in India. [122]

Any question about the impact of outsourcing on the US can be surmised by the rankings in *BusinessWeek's 2005* list of the Top 100 Info Tech Companies: India's Infosys was ranked 10th, Tata Consultancy 12th, Wipro 23rd, compared to Microsoft 27th, Accenture 31st, IBM 44th, and Intel 52nd. [597]

India Targets Our R&D Jobs

India's strategy was to start with low skill jobs, and then "move up the value chain" going after our strategic high tech jobs. [105] For example, in 2003, Rajesh Kishore, Gujarat's Secretary of Department of Science and Technology traveled to the US to persuade US companies to offshore IT, *biotechnology and pharmaceutical research.* His strategy was to *use financial and other incentives and to get help from India diaspora in to US to persuade US companies to offshore to India.* [318]

In 2005, Gartner predicted that offshore R&D and engineering would *grow 800% to $12 billion by 2010.* [122]

India Targets Our High Tech Manufacturing

India's Prime Minister said: *"Outsourcing of services is an outgrowth of outsourcing in manufacturing processes, which has been going on for quite some time,"* on the Charlie Rose show in September 2004. "*It is a logical byproduct of the era of globalization.*" He claimed sending US jobs to India helped American companies survive. [422]

By 2006 India felt *the time was ripe* to pursue manufacturing Information Technology hardware, according to an article, "Indian IT Manufacturing Takes Off," by Indrajit Basu. He found huge amounts of money were channeled into India to setup manufacturing capabilities. *Non-resident Indians (NRI's) living in Silicon Valley sent $3 billion. Also funding India's manufacturing build up* were US high tech companies: Cisco $1.14 billion, Microsoft $1.7 billion, and Intel $1 billion. [506]

India Targets Our Legal Industry

"Are Your Lawyers in New York or New Delhi?" a 2005 article said offshoring US legal work started in 1995. Following the typical pattern, *an immigrant from India living in the United States persuaded a Texas litigation firm to open an office in India.* Again the lure was "cost savings." Offshoring of legal work was forecasted to reach *$163 billion by 2006*. [479]

Outsourcing firms in India were not content with low level legal work. One firm claimed it drafted a *"brief for a U.S. Supreme Court case!"* It is high risk to offshore Supreme Court briefs. [479] Did foreign lawyers help draft the 2,000+ pages of Obamacare or other legislation?

When US law firms resisted offshoring writing patent applications, India outsourcing firms would scour through patent applications the US firms had filed. If errors were found, they would threaten to contact clients whose patents had errors–unless the US firms decided to offshore. [479]

"Bangalore's Big Dreams"

"If you think tech outsourcing is limited to call centers, software writing, and back office operations, think again. <u>The same Indian firms that generated the outsourcing wave—and the ensuing jobs controversy—are moving up what one executive calls the "value chain,"</u> reported a 2005, *US News & World Report*, "Bangalore's Big Dreams." [122]

Tata Consultancy Services, Infosys Technologies and Wipro began pursuing our advanced high tech jobs. They called this a *"silent revolution"* because unlike help-lines where Americans heard someone with an Indian accent, the American public would not have a clue of what is going on–*"anonymity is the rule."* This *"IT services revolution is only the opening act of a larger transformation,"* that is paving the way for offshoring US businesses to Asia. [122]

India's outsourcing companies maintained a high level of secrecy claiming that they are working on projects <u>*"they can't talk about for competitive reasons."*</u> [122] Under the shroud of secrecy, *no one knows what they are selling and to whom they are selling.* They may sell designs pirated from one US high tech company client to another US company and we wouldn't know, or to companies in India and we wouldn't know, or to China and we wouldn't know, or to terrorists and we wouldn't know. Because they are in a foreign country and because of the secrecy it is impossible to know. [122]

*"On any given day at Wipro and Infosys, welcome signs for visiting <u>clients read like a list of **America's best known corporations**,"</u>* the story reported. The firms want to be anonymous. However, a few of Wipro's 400 corporate clients includes: *"Morgan Stanley, Sun Microsystems, General Motors, Honeywell, Cisco, and Lucent."* [122]

Shockingly outsourcing companies in India were *"<u>remotely managing client's computer networks..</u>"* India's outsourcing companies were gaining access to US computers storing strategic valuable technology designs.

The report said the 1970s IBM dominated outsourcing. Then Azim Premij formed Wipro to compete against IBM. Premij's Wipro became *"a leading world provider of high tech services as the outsourcing wave gathered speed."* From 2001–2005 Wipro's revenues, *"nearly tripled"* reaching $1.9 billion making Premij, a Muslim who owned 84% of the company, the "richest man in India."

> Premij, who travels frequently to the US, *"says without complaint that he has been subjected to extra scrutiny by U.S. airport security."* Premij argued that the US economy benefits from *"efficiency and competitiveness when some jobs shift to lower-cost countries."* And, he was "proud that Wipro and its counterparts are boosting India's economy." [122]

Wipro talked about packaging a "Wipro brain" under other companies' names. "Design" projects mentioned included <u>altering an inexpensive computer chip to "mimic a pricey one"</u>. [122] Producing a knockoff of an expensive computer chip would require little skill if their network has access to the computer systems storing the design secrets of the chip they were to "mimic".

This article acknowledged a Deloitte Consulting report said <u>"major corporations are reassessing outsourcing in light of "significant negative experiences.""</u> [122]

Three years later a 2008 article, "India Rides Growth Wave Into New Age of Tech Globalization," in the *Electronic Engineering Times* claimed NASSCOM reported that *India's software and services exports were expected to reach $63 billion, and that <u>India's IT "growth is on track" to reach $73 billion by 2010</u>*. [673]

And sure enough, by 2010, outsourcing and offshoring by US firms such as Intel, Cisco, Google, IBM, and Microsoft had *transferred not only jobs, but $60 billion a year in IT revenues from the US to India*. [921]

BPO Summit in New Delhi

A World BPO Forum Summit was held in New Delhi, India in December 2006. It was an *invitation only event* for high level executives from international (American) companies interested in business process outsourcing (BPO). <u>Targeted industries were:</u> <u>*finance, accounting, insurance, customer relations, supply chain management*</u> <u>*and human resource management.*</u> [562]

■ *Vendors included India's outsourcing companies such as: Infosys, TCS, Wipro, Satyam, HCL.., along with American companies such as IBM and GE who sold BPO based in India.*

■ *Companies targeted for BPO included: Sara Lee, Kraft, Kellogg, Home Depot, Staples, Toys "R" Us, Kroger, Safeway, CVS, Levis Straus, Nike, Pfizer, Merck, Delta Airlines, Northwest Airlines, JetBlue, and many more.* [562]

India's Government Protectionist

US corporations did a double take in 2006. India demonstrated that it was protectionist of an industry that it did not create and only obtained access to through promoting "free trade." The Indian government re-imposed a levy of 12% (which had been removed in 2005), making imported computers more expensive, and added a tax credit to Indian manufacturers of computers allowing them to lower their prices.

India hardware manufacturers argued that this government protectionism was essential to *put them on equal footing with the type of government support that the Chinese manufacturers enjoy.* India and China are competing with each other over technology that was invented in the US and belongs to the US. [506]

And, who in our government is looking out for US manufacturing?

Suspicious Jump in Technology

Offshore outsourcing is like snake oil. It is sold as a remedy for all problems when in reality it does no good and dispossesses buyers of their money and other resources.

Recall we spent triple what China spent on R&D. Well, the gap with India is much bigger. *We spent 13 times more than India in 2009, and 11 times more in 2010 and 2011.* [990]

There should be no way that India could be even close to our technology advances. However, India's growth seems to track suspiciously close to our own. As if they have a direct connection into our proprietary research and databases storing our technology secrets.

We need to take back our jobs. Invest in US R&D done by Americans not by foreign students and visa workers. And we need to unplug India's "hardwired" connections to our Silicon Valley.

Chapter 16

Hidden Trade Deficit

Financial hocus pocus–now you see it, now you don't.

Our real trade deficit is much worse than is being reported. For example, in 2003 our worst trade deficits reported ran $124 billion with China; $66 billion with Japan, $54 billion with Canada, $40 billion with Mexico, and $39 billion with Germany. [177] Where was India–was a huge part of our deficit not reported?

Much of *hidden trade deficit is cunningly interwoven into financial reports as positive to our US Gross Domestic Product (GDP)*! For example, *money paid to foreign company subsidiaries operating inside the US is reported as a positive on our GDP.* So, India's outsourcing companies operations in the US are counted as positive to our GDP even though they displaced Americans and had a negative impact in our overall economy.

Other money flows from the US to foreign sources that are not included in our trade deficit calculations are: foreign aid, foreign investments, offshoring by US banks, money transfers, and more. A 2011, analysis of our 2009 assistance to "developing" countries included $28.8 billion in economic development aid paid by our taxes, plus $37.5 billion in private giving, and $69.2 billion in private investment. But that's not all, foreigners *working in the United States sent and astounding $90.7 billion in money transfers to their home countries!* [997] The book False Prophets of False Profits shows how reducing or eliminating these transfers is essential to our economic recovery.

China's Piece of the Hidden Deficit

US companies spent billions building production and research facilities in China. For example, in 2005, _EETimes_ reported that a group named CMD International (Tianjin) Electronic Co. Ltd., was planning to spend more than $2.5 billion to build a huge semiconductor plant, and a research center in China. The article also noted that _although the CMD group was very low profile it included several large integrated circuit (IC) companies in Silicon Valley_. [474]

China's banks sought money from US banks. For example, in 2006 the Industrial & Commercial Bank of China Ltd, (ICBC) one of China's four large _state-owned commercial banks_ was the third of China's banks to sell shares to investors in other countries. The goal was to raise $19 billion. _These banks linked up with American and European banking partners to obtain capital_. [584]

China aggressively sought _US venture capital to fund its build up_. For example, China's Comtech Group was described as "_a gateway to leading electronics manufacturers in China._" Comtech presented at a 2005 Needham & Company LLC "_Growth Conference_" in New York to _find investors_ so it could expand from telecom into "_consumer electronics end-markets._" [449]

When China persuaded US companies to offshore production of consumer electronic products, it became a major buyer of chips used in electronic products. So the next year China was positioned to go after our chip industry. Needham's analysts in 2006 forecasted 40% gross margins and 20% net margins for investors in Chinese fabless IC manufacturers, according to a "Confab: Chips, China Good Investments," _EETimes_ article. This "_Growth Conference_," said _American IC companies could not provide these investment margins because of higher costs for labor, legal, and accounting expenses_. Besides, they said _Chinese electronics manufacturers prefer to buy chips made in China_. [447]

Interestingly, Needham also advised our government to use incentives to persuade companies to invest in the US instead of overseas. And, it advised _keeping H-1B visa workers in the US because when H-1Bs return to their country_ **_many US jobs go with them_**. [447]

You may know that the Chinese government subsidizes Chinese businesses selling in America. However, did you know that our government is subsidizing Chinese businesses as well by using our taxes to fund inspections, education of students, designs, insure banks and more. (Also see Democracy Hijacked book to learn about how our tax funded foreign aid was financing foreign competition.)

Moreover, our government has taxed us to fund research done in foreign countries. One appalling example, _foxnews.com_ reported: "NIH funds $2.6 Million Study to Get Prostitutes in China to Drink Less." Dr. Xiaoming Li of Wayne State University who was conducting the study did not respond to _Fox News'_ emails. However, he told _CNS News_ that the study was to assess how alcohol use related to HIV risk. He thought, "the findings will benefit the American people, too." [988]

How many more R&D projects like this are being funded by our taxes? Given our trade deficit with China it is outrageous for us to fund research in China. It is not possible for our country to be the technology leader if our government funds research done in foreign nations by foreign workers.

So, money you invested in US stocks, and saved in US banks was misdirected by executives to fund China's buildup. Money you paid in taxes was used by our government to fund China's buildup. Do our "investments" in China's build up exceed the amount of US treasuries and other US assets China holds? Congress needs to compute what China owes so we can buy back US treasuries and US assets.

India Worse than China

The source of 44% of money transfers to India came from North America in 2003. *Diaspora in the US sent an estimated $10 billion a year back home to India.* The Reserve Bank of India cleverly labeled transfers the "*Invisibles in India's Balance of Payments.*" [616] The Middle East supplied $24%. [616]

In a "The Role of the Diaspora" speech Professor Jagdish Bhagwati said *remittances diaspora sent "home" to India had grown to $41 billion in 2007-2008.* But even that was not enough; he wanted diaspora with dual US citizenship to pay "*a Bhagwati tax*" to India "*their mother country.*" He said diaspora build up India, and connects India with scientific research. [887]

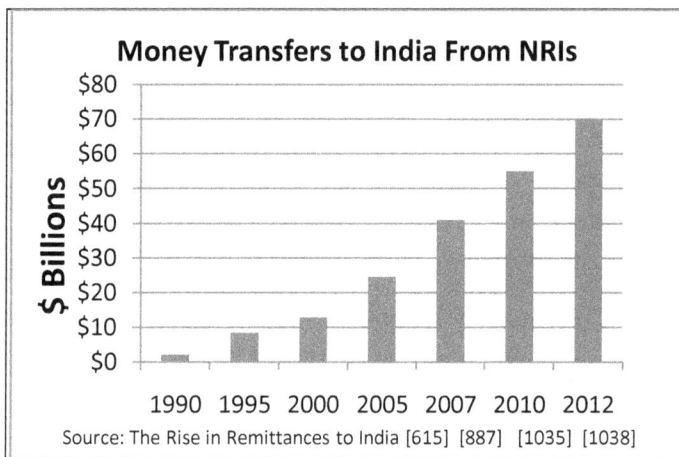

Money Transfers to India From NRIs

Source: The Rise in Remittances to India [615] [887] [1035] [1038]

Of worldwide 2010 remittances, India received $55 billion, China $51 billion and Mexico $23 billion. The biggest loser was *our country which lost $48 billion!* [1035] Our real losses are worse because the official counts don't include money in socks, backpacks, and briefcases crossing our border. It is estimated that the real number may be "50% higher." [1032]

Remittances received in 2012 ran India $70 billion, China $66 billion, and Mexico $24 billion.

US Venture Capital Channeled to India

<u>*Our country was the source of about 80% of India's venture capital.*</u> *TiE was connected to 40% of the venture capital investment in India in 2001-2002.* In a New Delhi news release, "The TiE That Binds Could Bring in $800M by 2006," Saurabha Srivastava, a founding member of *The Indus Entrepreneurs* (TiE), and president of the *Indian Venture Capital Association* (IVCA) said that 400 of TiE's 600 charter members were "angel investors" funding IT, telecom, and BPO companies in India. [652]

And then in 2005, a scheme was hatched where venture capital firms required US IT startups to use software developers in India claiming this would slow *"cash burn rates."* [407] What is really being "burned" is our leadership in technology as US citizens are forced to transfer innovations offshore if they needed venture capital money.

(Also see next Chapter on how banks got involved in venture capital investments and moved money offshore.)

Hotmail – Anonymous email

Hotmail was created by Sabeer Bhatia and Jack Smith. The story goes that when Jack called Sabeer on a cell-phone to discuss the idea Sabeer exclaimed, *"Oh, my! Hang up the cellular and call me back on a secure line when you get to your house! We don't want anyone to overhear!"* Sabeer knew technology thieves were listening in on US phone calls. Apparently Jack didn't know. [585] What was so secret? The idea was to set up free anonymous emails that could be sent over the Internet from work without being seen by US employers. Company email was not anonymous and personal email accounts could not be accessed at work.

Was Hotmail used as a tool to steal US technology secrets from US corporations by attaching copied files to anonymous emails sent to foreign companies?

Corruption Costs Billions

We need to shine the light to expose the hidden deficit. It does not make sense for us to send aid or give financial support to nations we owe money. Instead we should make payments to pay off our debt. Of course, we should only do this after an audit is done to determine what we really owe. We should not reimburse patent infringements, counterfeiting, and/or other crimes.

We need to reevaluate funding the UN, the World Bank and other international or foreign recipients.

It is time to pick leaders who will limit the money transfers that foreign workers can send to foreign countries. Anyone in our country illegally should not be able to transfer money out of our country.

Chapter 17

Risky Offshoring by US Banks

Banks are gambling with our money.

American banks that morphed into multinationals were taking money out of circulation in the United States by making high risk business loans in foreign countries.

Bankers get rich by paying you low interest rates, and then charging very high interest rates for high risk investments.

A December 2006, press release announced that the chief executive of Goldman Sachs took a record setting $53.4 million bonus. A group of eleven more senior executives at Goldman took over $150 million in shares and stock options. The money came from a surge in takeovers where the stock valuation rose 58%. [564]

Bankers were gambling with our money. For example, in the 1980's, NationsBank suffered major losses when it invested in banks in Brazil and Argentina. [116] In 1999, twenty two percent of Chase's net income came from high risk venture capital investments. [355]

And, in 2005, Bank of America abandoned its policy of domestic only banking and bought $3 billion of the China Construction Bank even though other banks found the level of risk unacceptable. [183]

Offshoring Investment Services & Research

Financial companies, such as JP Morgan Chase and American Express, also offshored. [116] JP Morgan Chase was criticized for obtaining taxpayer funded contracts then offshoring the work to India and Mexico. Its Financial Services division had contracts for supporting welfare programs and food stamps for over 30 states in America. It also has an investment banking division that employed researchers in India. [6] So researchers in India are recommending investments.

In 2003, major *US banks such as Morgan Stanley, Goldman Sachs Group and Citigroup were offshoring research jobs to India.* They could hire ten analysts in India for the cost of one American analyst. [63] [89] [117] Using foreign analysts may pump up bankers bonuses, but it also poses unacceptable risks and conflicts of interest. Banks should have to report who did an analysis.

Financial Crisis

US banks that morphed into multinationals wanted Americans to bail them out in 2009. Americans objected. The US Congress passed the Troubled Asset Relief Program (TARP) "stimulus" bill anyway. Why?

A 2009 OpenSecrets report discovered that *"TARP Recipients Paid Out $114 Million Politicking Last Year."* Over 300 companies received money from TARP. The companies that spent the most money on campaigns and lobbying got the most money. On its website, *www.opensecrets.org* the companies are named and graphics analyze the data. [738] Congress did not even make sure these banks would not channel TARP money outside the US.

It is unjust to ask you to bail out banks that converted into multinationals. These companies went offshore to evade paying their fair share of US taxes. And, they harmed Americans by displacing them with foreign workers.

Indian Outsourcing Debarment Cover-up Exposed

"Exclusive: World Bank's Web of Ties to 'India's Enron'" by *foxnews.com* in 2009 reported *three Indian outsourcing companies, Satyam, Megasoft, and Wipro, were debarred by the World Bank*. One of the most disturbing aspects of the report was that *World Bank officials concealed the corruption for over three years and pressured the Government Accountability Project to "keep the information under wraps."* [722]

World Bank officials *"felt no obligation to the global corporate community to share that information publicly until late last month."* Unaware American corporations *"entrusted their most sensitive computer networks"* to these outsourcing companies. By 2009, *more than 150 Fortune 500 companies such as Citicorp, General Electric, Microsoft, Nestle, Dell, and Merrill Lynch* were listed as Satyam clients when Satyam "imploded" in a $1 billion accounting fraud. [722]

- *The Bank banned Satyam in 2007 after it found that "preferential Satyam shares" were received by the Bank's Chief Information Officer Mohamed Muhsin. The Bank kept Satyam's employees by converting them into employees of Tata (another Indian outsourcing company.) and EDS. This was shocking given the corruption and the discovery that a Satyam employee had "implanted spyware in the bank's systems."* [722]

- *In 2005, the Bank awarded Wipro a $650,000 contract for providing shareholders protection through financial transparency. In 2007, Wipro was banned from doing business with the Bank when Bank officials learned that Wipro sold "Friends and Family" shares to Muhsin. The bank also banned Muhsin.* [722]

Were these *"preferential shares,"* and *"friends and family"* shares tactics also used to obtain contracts with US CEOs and politicians? Such collusive means to get contracts not based on the best quality and best cost, but rather based on bribes is highly destructive.

Offshoring Americans' Financial Data

In 2004, Oracle decided to double the size of its research centers in Hyderabad and Bangalore to 6,000 employees. [6] Also in 2004, Oracle did a hostile takeover of PeopleSoft. *This acquisition doubled Oracle's customer base. Oracle wanted to dominate the applications market for US banking, and strengthen its position in the US health care industry and US government.* [162] Our government unsuccessfully attempted to block this takeover in court. [163] Why was the US government unable to stop this risky takeover? How do you feel about workers in foreign countries being able to go through your personal private financial data?

American Banks Should be American Banks

American banks should be American owned and employ Americans. We cannot regulate banks in other countries. Nor can we afford to insure multinational banks. The US can only pass and enforce laws in the United States. It is far too dangerous to allow bankers controlling Americans' money, to operate outside the jurisdiction of our legal system. They may use our money to fund foreign competition and harm our economy, or they may use our money to fund companies or countries that pose national security or military threats.

Chapter 18

Risks of Foreign 'Investors'

Disguised to cover up true identity.

Pseudo US corporations are used to camouflage the growing threat of foreign takeover of American high tech industries. While they are officially registered as US corporations, these companies employ many foreign workers, and may have more foreign employees than Americans. These "US companies" are shells for selling foreign made products and services in the US.

Pseudo US corporations are created when:

- *Executives hire H-1Bs and lay off US citizens.*

- *US corporations convert into multinational corporations and begin "transferring" production, services, and research to foreign countries.*

- *Foreign buyers acquire US corporations.*

- *Startups formed as US corporations, are staffed with H-1Bs and offshore workers. Many recent immigrants founded "US corporations" that fall into this category.*

We need to define what it takes to be an American company. For example, if a company's employees are one quarter foreigners, is it still an American company? If a company sells technology secrets to foreign competition jeopardizing our economy and/or national security, is it still an American company?

Foreign Investment Threat

In the short term, foreign investment may appear beneficial because the influx of money stimulates our economy. However, there are many factors that make the risks of some foreign investment outweigh the benefits. Instead of venture capital, it may be better labeled "vulture capital."

First, it matters where the money comes from that is invested. It is highly destructive to allow people who obtained money selling pirated US goods, illegal drugs, abusing workers, or exploiting children, etcetera to invest in our country.

Second, foreign investments can be used to control our politicians and business leaders by threatening to withdraw the money and harm our economy.

Third, foreign investors can pressure US executives to convert US corporations into multinational corporations. They can pressure executives to hire foreign workers and promote foreign nationals into executive ranks. The concept is like using a cup of water to prime a pump. A few million dollars are invested in a US corporation, then billions of dollars worth of technology and future earnings are pumped out i.e. stolen.

Fourth, foreign investors may manipulate our stock market. They may use pump and dump or other illegal means to manipulate stock and rob American investors.

Fifth, foreign investors may purposely make a US startup fail so they can seize and transfer new technology to a foreign startup.

It also matters where our money goes. Money may be used to finance foreign militaries that threaten the US or other nations. It may be used to finance foreign corporations that will compete against US businesses in the US market and abroad.

Venture Firm Monopoly Risks

Venture capital firms can invest in multiple companies within the same industry. Or a wealthy individual investor or group of investors may be involved in multiple venture capital firms. So it is not a corporate monopoly, but rather an individual or group exercising monopoly power.

Multi Industry Monopolies

Large corporations, and/or billionaires may branch out and gain influential control of multiple industries. For example, look at how GE acquired major media interests, while also being a government contractor, while outsourcing to India. Through acquiring control of our media, a company is in the position to promote positive media to stock investors and to suppress negative media coverage such as criticisms of layoffs, outsourcing, offshoring, executive compensation, and more.

Foreign "Investments" Reform

Foreign investments create many obvious and many not so obvious risks. Foreign investments need to be carefully monitored, controlled, and regulated. For example, we need boundaries and limits set on what they can buy and how much they can buy.

Chapter 19

Foreign Acquisitions of US

Assets

Selling our future

When we bought foreign made products and services, foreign nations gained enormous buying power. China, India, and other nations leveraged cheap labor to devour US technology secrets and buy up US businesses and US real estate. *Foreign ownership of US assets jumped from 8.8% in 1987 to 26% in 2005!* [495] A 2011 World Bank report *predicted that by 2025 foreign ownership of US assets would increase 5 fold! The biggest buyers-"Emerging Asian countries."* [1009]

Every time our money flows to foreign nations, it negatively impacts our real trade deficit unless it is offset by an equal inflow of money. Whether our money goes to foreign companies, the UN, the World Bank, foreign charities..., the money eventually returns to the US to make purchases. Some people claim that it is good for foreign countries to have US dollars because then they can buy products and services from us thereby creating American jobs.

However, countries such as China, India, Mexico, and others where labor is much cheaper than in the US, rarely purchase products or services made by Americans. Instead, they prefer to use US dollars to purchase: US corporations, US real estate, US intellectual property, US Treasury securities, US political influence, US media, and other US assets.

"Selling Our Country Out from Under Us"!

Ben Franklin warned about the perils of debt: *"Think what you do when you run in debt; you give to another power over your liberty."*

Some "experts" claimed we should not worry about foreign acquisitions because the money is not in the form of loans that the US has to repay, but rather in the form of foreign purchasing of US assets such as US companies, US real estate and US stocks. The theory is that these foreign buyers depend on the US economy doing well to protect the value of the assets. [488] However, some intelligent people do not ascribe to this theory.

In a 2003 article in *Fortune* that Warren Buffett co-wrote with Carol J. Loomis, "America's Growing Trade Deficit is Selling The Nation Out From Under Us. Here's a Way to Fix the Problem – And We Need to Do It Now," Buffett warned, *"our trade deficit has greatly worsened, to the point that <u>our country's "net worth" so to speak, is being transferred abroad at an alarming rate</u>."* Buffett estimated foreigners may acquire $500 billion in US assets annually. [160]

Foreign nations bought US Treasury securities to artificially prop up the debt to camouflage the full extent of the damage to our economy and to unfairly tilt trade in their favor.

By 2005, foreigners held over $2 trillion of the $4 trillion outstanding US Treasury securities. [570] [499]

Incredulously a Wall Street Journal article "White House Aims to Lure More Foreign Investment," reported in 2011 that Obama planned to seek $1 Trillion in foreign investments. [963] Such a strategy will self destruct our country.

By late 2011 foreigners held $5.48 trillion of our Treasury securities! China was the biggest holder with 1.16 trillion, followed by Japan with $1.13 trillion. [1042]

Some Things Should Not Be Sold

Most Americans would be surprised to learn that about 80% of US ports are now foreign managed. [497] US ports are considered prime targets for terrorists or foreign governments to use to smuggle counterfeit products, people and weapons of mass destruction into the US. [498] Foreign companies were allowed to buy and lease US roads and bridges that were built using taxpayer money when federal highway funds were depleted. Imagine foreign companies charging Americans tolls to drive in our own country. Our leaders even allowed foreign companies to buy control of over 10% of US drinking water. [499]

Some things should never be foreign owned or controlled-our government, our ports, our highways and our water probably fall into that category for most Americans.

Buying US Companies to Eliminate US Competitors

Foreigners may acquire a US corporation not with the intent to make it profitable, but rather with the intent to eliminate American competition. They close down the US operations. And, as an added bonus the foreign acquirers claim US investment "losses" they can take tax write offs–even though they intentionally caused the losses. Moreover, since the "transfer" process can take several years, they deceitfully appeal to our government for more US taxpayer funded R&D to "keep the US globally competitive." As new technology is developed it is "transferred" out of the US for foreign production.

Acquisitions to Funnel Illegal Products into USA

Acquiring American companies can allow foreign nations to channel products into the US illegally and sell them in retail stores. This makes it much more difficult to screen for illegal products.

Foreign Acquisitions to Immigrate

Foreign acquisitions of American companies allow foreigners to immigrate to America. Once a US company is acquired, they can begin applying for visa applications and bringing in foreign workers.

Foreign Government Sovereign-Wealth Funds

CBS News ran a story about how the US mortgage and credit crisis had gotten so bad during the winter of 2007-2008, that Wall Street mega-banks were driven to seek tens of billions of dollars from foreign government controlled sovereign-wealth funds. At issue was whether these foreign governments such as Abu Dhabi and Kuwait, were bailing the US out of a financial crisis, *or were they "gobbling up" US companies.* [684]

The fund of greatest concern was China's *"new, highly secretive"* five month old China Investment Corporation headquartered in Beijing. This fund, already the "fifth largest in the world" spent billions in 2007 buying up investment houses on Wall Street. The fund bought "over $100 million worth of shares in Visa." China's fund manager warned that it would be *"a problem emotionally"* if the US attempted to pass laws governing the conduct of sovereign-wealth funds, *"That law will only hurt feelings."*

One economist warned that *"China has so much money that they can spend buying U.S. companies that the danger is that they can strip these companies...of jobs, research and development, technology."* [684]

To get its way China can threaten to dump its US investments–the *"financial nuclear option."* [684] China held $1.5 trillion in reserves and the Chinese government held half a trillion dollars worth of US Treasury bonds.

How did China get so much US money – outsourcing by American companies in combination *with "unfair trade practices, currency manipulation, technology espionage ...and counterfeiting."* [684]

Foreign Acquisitions Multiplier Effect

When a foreign company acquires a US company it can have a multiplier damaging effect. It gives the foreign company the power to go onsite to visit American suppliers' operations enabling espionage. Then they then can transfer the knowledge and eliminate the American suppliers. For example, if a Chinese company acquires an American computer manufacturer, it can then replace American computer chip supplier and other computer component suppliers with Chinese suppliers. So, one strategic purchase can harm thousands of US companies.

Multiplier Effect Model™ of Damage to US
Caused by Foreign Acquisition of a US Company

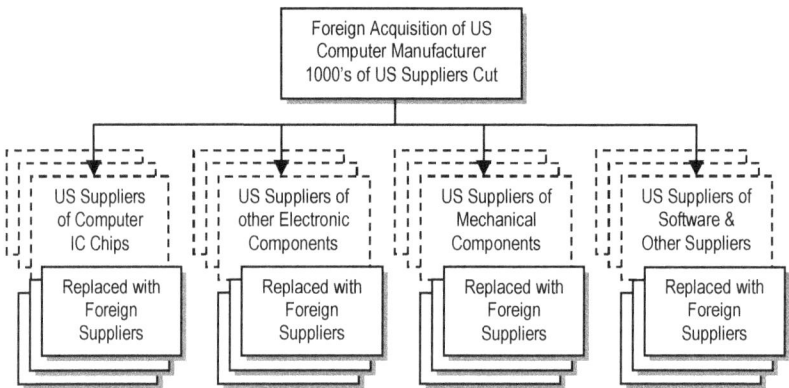

Jeffery Immelt was the CEO of GE and also "head of the White House Council on Jobs and Competitiveness in 2011. He tried to justify GE offshoring saying GE moved to China, India, and more "because that's where the customers are." Yet, as was noted in a *USA Today* article, *"those customers Immelt refers to are multinationals that did move factories abroad for cheap labor and which need GE there to supply them."* [923]

Acquiring Military Contractors

It is vital that US military secrets not fall into foreign government hands. [233] *By 2002, a takeover trend began engulfing US military contractors.* [135] As acquisitions and mergers continued, there were fewer government contractors and corruption increased. What was our government doing to prevent foreign acquisitions of these contractors?

China Acquiring American Companies

In May 1997, a special report warned that according to a *BusinessWeek* article *about 100 Chinese owned companies had cunningly maneuvered to acquire a select list of American companies that allowed them to clandestinely gain access to our financial markets.*

The article told how the Chinese PLA was strategically buying successful American companies with the *intent to obtain American technology secrets for transfer to China.* As an example, the article claimed Sunbase Asia, Inc. acquired Southwest Products Company a manufacturer of specialized bearings used by all major American aircraft manufacturers, and used in US government applications such as the space shuttle and military transport. According to the report Sunbase executives *"made no secret of the fact that they plan to transfer the bearings technology from California to the Chinese bearings company."* [173]

In 2005, China attempted to buy Unocal the ninth largest US oil company. China needed a loan for a billion dollars to finance the purchase. China claimed that they planned to protect US jobs and market products in the US. Americans protested this attempt by a Chinese government controlled corporation to buy an American oil company.

This was only one of many aggressive mergers and acquisitions of US energy pursued by Chinese companies. [180]

Indian Firms "Acquisition Spree" of US Companies

India limits *"foreign ownership in industries such as defense, news media, retail and some forms of banking,"* according to a 2005 *BusinessWeek* article, "Private Equity Pours Into India," [721] Yet they targeted these and other industries for US acquisitions.

India went after our telecom industry so that it could increase offshore outsourcing of US jobs–Ironically, we enabled them when *"$30 billion in U.S. owned international telecom infrastructure had been sold for about $4 billion."* India said, *"the timing of this transaction is well suited to our international expansion plans"* [590] For instance a 2004, article, "India's Tata Group Acquires Tyco Network at Bargain Price," said Tata acquired *"the world's most advanced and extensive submarine cable system"* valued at $3 billion before the dotcom crash for only $130 million.

India also targeted our US defense contractors. For example, in 2005, INDUS Corporation acquired AB Floyd Enterprises, a privately held IT company that provided services to the US Department of Defense and to US intelligence clients. INDUS CEO Shiv Krishnan said: *"It fits our strategy of becoming a full-service IT solutions provider for all Federal customers, including national defense and intelligence sectors."* [592]

"Indian Companies are on an Acquisition Spree: Their Target: U.S. Firms," a 2006 article reported that, *Indian companies acquired strategic American companies including: IT, pharmaceutical, chemical, healthcare, biotech, telecom, energy, steel and more. Their strategy is to buy "well-known brand" name companies that Americans trust.* [681]

A 2007 Wikipedia post, "Non-Resident Indian and Person of Indian Origin," said *NRIs acquired 35% of US hotels and 50% of US economy lodges worth a combined estimated real estate value of $40 billion.* [618] Were US hotels bought to house foreign students from India, H-1Bs from India, illegal aliens from India, or spies?

Outsourcing = Cunningly Clever Takeover

Outsourcing was a cunningly clever way to take over American companies. Instead of buying the company; they got paid. They moved up the value chain taking programming jobs, then accounting jobs, then management jobs—before long they had control of the company. Outsourcing spreads its tentacles like kudzu. At first it looked like a good idea. But it rapidly spreads slithering up beautiful trees and then destroys the structure supporting them. Ultimately the US company collapses and is replaced by a foreign company to avoid paying US shareholders. H-1Bs keep channeling new US technology offshore.

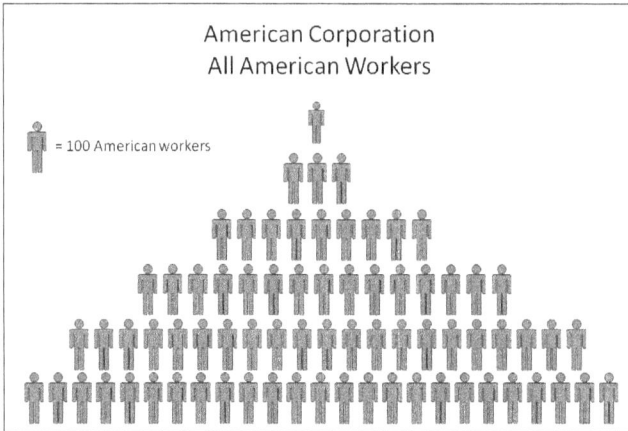

American Corporation
All American Workers

= 100 American workers

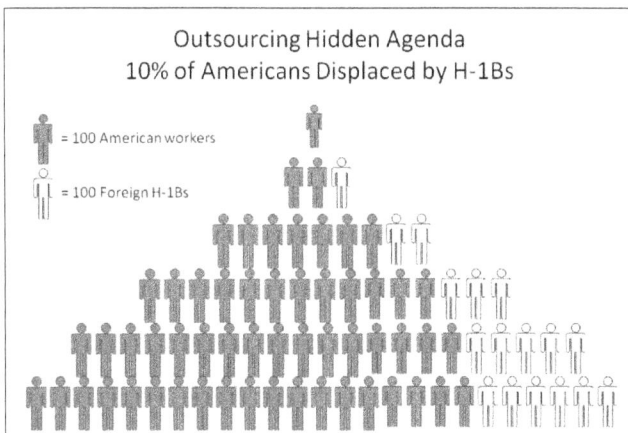

Outsourcing Hidden Agenda
10% of Americans Displaced by H-1Bs

= 100 American workers

= 100 Foreign H-1Bs

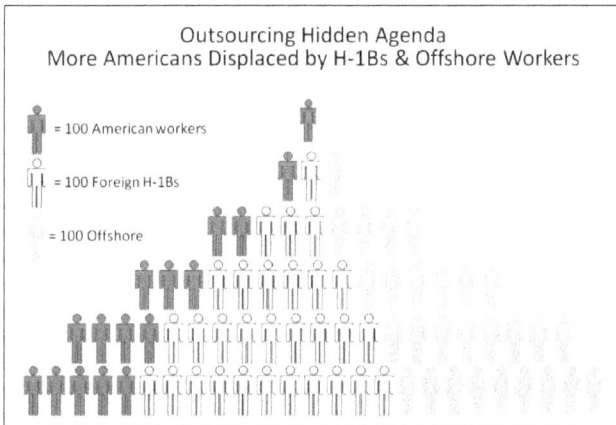

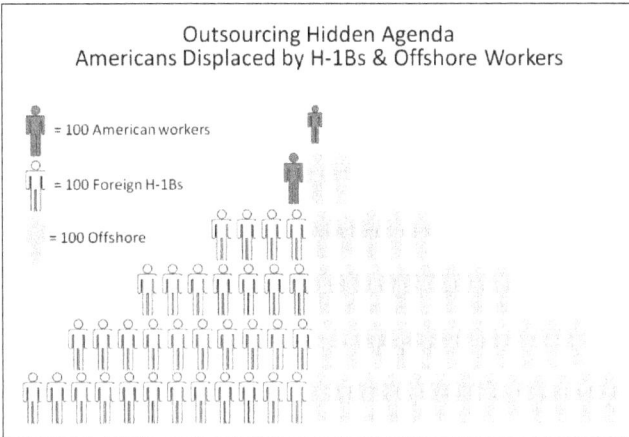
Outsourcing Hidden Agenda
Americans Displaced by H-1Bs & Offshore Workers

= 100 American workers
= 100 Foreign H-1Bs
= 100 Offshore

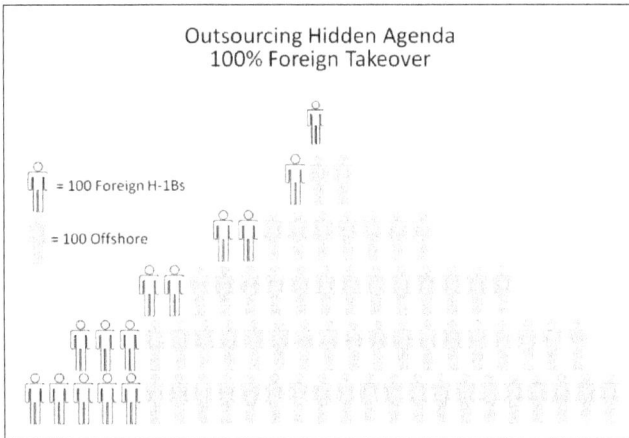
Outsourcing Hidden Agenda
100% Foreign Takeover

= 100 Foreign H-1Bs
= 100 Offshore

Outsourcing Hidden Agenda
'NEW' Foreign Company Keeps H-1Bs in US

= 100 Foreign H-1Bs
= 100 Foreign

Middle East Acquiring US Technology

The Middle East is also seeking to acquire <u>advanced US chip technology</u>. According to a 2008, article, "Dubai: From Sand to Silicon," Dubai was preparing to "<u>build a new Silicon Valley from scratch</u>." This "technology city" expected to have a population of 150,000 people, with 25,000 of these being engineers. Dubai attracted companies from around the world with "zero personal and corporate taxes." [707] Some of the money came from external investors. This may include money from terrorists. And, the expertise is supplied by US "partnership deals" with organizations such as: "*the Rochester Institute of Technology.*" [707]

Where was Our Government?

Why were young Americans fighting a war for our country while it was being "sold out from under us?" We need better leaders.

Chapter 20

Privacy Invasion on a Global Scale

"The right of people to be secure in their persons, houses, papers, and effects, against unreasonable searches and seizures, shall not be violated, and no warrants shall issue, but upon probable cause, supported by oath or affirmation, and particularly describing the place to be searched, and the persons or things to be seized." [412]

4th Amendment

The fourth Amendment guarantees our privacy rights.

Companies claimed that they gathered information on you so that they can better serve customers. However, renowned economist *John Kenneth Galbraith analyzed the "market driven system" propaganda. He determined that the massive amount of data being gathered on American consumers was not done to benefit consumers, but rather to control and manage you.* [1]

Additionally, offshoring escalates the risk of identity theft to a global scale. If a foreign worker in a foreign country violates your privacy, it may be difficult if not impossible for you to obtain damages. Many countries where Business Process Outsourcing (BPO) is being done do not have privacy laws, or may lack the motivation or ability to effectively enforce privacy laws.

Your Most Private Data Offshored!

The range of jobs US companies offshored included: *credit card services, debit card services, financial data, payroll processing, loan administration, student loans processing, bill collection, medical transcription, medical insurance claims processing, analyzing CAT scans, US tax return preparation, legal database processing, employment screening, employee benefits, consumer analysis, customer support, and more.* [77] [63] [105]

In 2000, an article "How Companies Court Disaster in Outsourcing Deals" warned that companies need to better understand the risks of BPO. [133] The US was the prime target for India's BPO drive because *European countries had tighter controls on data security.* [105]

Offshore BPO work is dominated by India: *"Indian staffs troll the private medical and financial records of U.S. consumers to help determine if they are good risks for insurance policies, mortgages, or credit cards from American Express Co. and J.P Morgan Chase & Co."* [300]

- In 2004, American Express was ranked number seven on a list of India's biggest BPO customers. American Express had laid off thousands of Americans while it was busy hiring around 3,500 employees in India and an unknown number in the Philippines. [6]

- In 2004, a call center worker in India was caught trying to use a US citizen's credit card. [92]

- In 2003, a disgruntled Pakistani medical transcription worker threatened to reveal confidential medical data on American hospital patients. [146]

In 2003 Congress began a probe to determine if the security of American financial and medical records were jeopardized by offshore outsourcing. [300] In 2004 some politicians realized the privacy risks and planned to draft proposals to restrict offshore BPO. [146]

Caught Improperly Keeping Records

Tracking your credit card transactions beyond the need to process payments is invasive. It is very risky to have our credit scores accessed and maintained by foreign workers. [145

Credit cards purchases tell where you shop, when you shop, what you buy, how much money you spend, airline tickets you purchase, hotels where you've made reservations, and more. Companies are maintaining records on you that they are not supposed to be collecting. For example, in July 2005, an article, "Lost Credit Data Improperly Kept, Company Admits" revealed that a credit card company had violated customers' privacy. As a result when its security was breached *40 million of its credit card customers were put at risk.* [150]

Your internet service provider may also be violating your privacy.

A 2006, article, "AOL: Breach of Privacy was a Mistake," exposed that AOL released records on 650,000 of its subscribers for academic research analysis. Although AOL had substituted ID numbers instead of names, when searching online you may enter data that can be used to identify you. Privacy groups point out that *recording and tracking your Internet searches is a major invasion of privacy*. Internet search engines may gather private information such as your bank accounts, your medical records, your travel plans, personal interests, and much more. [554]

Online job application sites may also violate your privacy. A 2001 article, "Privacy Group Alleges Monster-ous Breach" claimed that *Monster.com* had not fully disclosed to American job hunters how their personal data might be used. It said that some data was distributed without the knowledge or consent of the American job seekers. [555]

Offshore Access to Your Bank Accounts

For many Americans setting up offshore access to their bank accounts offered zero benefit, and unacceptable exposure to theft. Americans probably do not want their bank accounts accessible in foreign countries where they rarely if ever travel. Experts expect fraud risks to be much greater in offshore operations. For example, in 2006, three people who had worked as contract employees in India were arrested accused of stealing $350,000 from CitiBank's US customers. [480]

Several major American banks offshored customer support and transaction processing. A few examples:

■ *Bank of America offshored consumer and corporate customer accounts to India. [90] Bank of America later acquired MBNA for $34 billion to gain control of 40 million Americans' credit card accounts. The plan was to cut 6,000 jobs which was supposed to result in $850 million in cost savings by 2007. [149] [148]*

■ *The Bank of New York offshored jobs to India and the Philippines.*

■ *Morgan Stanley offshored IT jobs to India and the Philippines.*

■ *Citigroup purchased an IT service company in India to manage its databases, transactions processing, and customer support calls. [6]*

■ *SunTrust, JP Morgan Chase, and Wachovia also offshored work.*

Identity Theft Risks

Identity theft can ruin your life by creating false information about you that impacts your ability to buy a home or find a job. In 2003, *ten million Americans were the victims of identity theft* at a cost of almost $50 billion. As a result, in 2004, President Bush signed a law that would send people convicted of identity theft to prison. Bush said identity theft crime *"undermines the basic trust on which our economy depends."* [152] However, offshoring increases identity theft risks, and this law cannot be enforced in a foreign country. [94]

Chapter 21

Big Brother Threat

"The time is now near at hand which must probably determine whether Americans are to be freemen or slaves; <u>whether they are to have any property they can call their own</u>; whether their houses and farms are to be pillaged and destroyed, and themselves consigned to a state of wretchedness from which no human efforts will deliver them."–George Washington

Did you know that US political campaigns are combing through your private data stored in databases to craft messages targeting you. <u>*This began under Bush during the 2004 election*</u>. At that time India was worried since our Defense Department and other government agencies sounded security alarms and wanted to stop using foreign programmers to process payroll, emails, and more. Bush reassured India that if he was elected that outsourcing would continue. Did foreign programmers help create the database that gave Bush the advantage?

The political databases get more invasive each election.

<u>*Obama also reassured India outsourcing would continue,*</u> and like Bush, *"Obama's voter database"* gave him an edge in 2008 and 2012. Development of his 2012 campaign database began 2 years before our election. It <u>*tracked your voting records and political donation history. It estimated whether you were likely to vote and if you lived in a "swing state." It was "capable of storing hundreds of fields on each voter." Imagine how this data could be used!*</u> His campaign database even gathered Facebook data to profile you and to "score" how well your friends like you. [1063]

"*Obama was able to collect and use personal data largely free of the restrictions that govern similar efforts by private companies.*" Why? Because "*Neither the Federal Trade Commission... nor the Federal Election Commission have jurisdiction over how campaigns use such information.*" [1063]

Most disturbing of all, these databases are considered <u>crucial for winning elections *after voting starts*</u>. If a vote isn't going how they want, they start calling people to go vote.

"Obama to Use Re-Election Machine to Target NRA," was a Jan 2013 breitbart.com report. The article told how "*Obama set his lackeys at Media Matters and Color of Change on the American Legislative Council (ALEC)*", when it tried to get voter ID laws passed. And that because of the "*Obama-led assault*" ALEC lost members who feared becoming targets also. It told how Obama tries "*to destroy political opponents.*" The article said that in his second term Obama "*sees no need to hide behind Media Matters any longer,*" and will "*go after all of his enemies, the NRA included.*" And that Obama will use the "*vast infrastructure he's built.*" [1065] However, Obama didn't build the network, nor did he build the database. If you didn't vote for him, or if you gave money to an opponent will he "*go after*" you?

These intrusive databases used by Bush and Obama jeopardize the integrity of our elections and harm "middle class folks" politicians claim to care about.

Outcomes from the three elections where they were deployed benefited foreign nations and foreign workers to the detriment of Americans and our national security. This should be investigated. And, these databases should be dismantled and outlawed.

The Chinese Communist government keeps detailed files on its people so that it can control them: "*the Chinese people are watched, monitored, and kept under surveillance from the day of birth to the grave.*" This is not supposed to happen in America. However: "<u>*Ominously, the U.S. government is now compiling similar records on most adult citizens in dozens of different computer data bases.*</u>" [173]

There are laws that prohibit our government from tracking our private activities. Yet, a 2004 article, "Panel Seeks Protections from Data Mining," reported The General Accounting Office discovered 54 government agencies bought data from aggregators. [402] Aggregators are companies that collect and link together your records and your family's records to create master databases. [402]

After the 9/11 attack, Oracle and Sun Microsystems, wanted to build a national ID card system for tracking Americans even though none of the terrorists were Americans. [193]

Legislation passed by the Senate in 2004 allows *local, state and federal governments and commercial computer systems to all be networked together for information sharing.* [159] That year our government also paid a company $100 million to develop a database tracking travelers–supposedly to catch terrorist. But, it was blocked for being *intrusive into the privacy of ordinary US citizens.* So the developer, a former US intelligence officer, moved his company to the Bahamas outside the reach of US laws. [159]

Do you, like most Americans, consider your medical data private? "Obamacare HHS Rule Would Give Government Everybody's Health Records," a 2011 *washingtonexaminer.com* report warned that "*government bureaucrats would have access to the health records of every American – including you.*" Obamacare controls the money, which means *it controls who gets care and how much.* [1006]

Obama sealed his school records, yet your information may be more open than you know. For example, software for creating databases that link student transcripts, to interviews, to soliciting donations, and more was sold by Intelliworks to universities including: The Wharton School, Duke University, Northwestern University's Kellogg School of Management, MIT, and more. [592]

Data from social networking sites has already been used by China to enable cyber attacks on US computers.

Our founding fathers would never believe what is going on in America. This is extremely dangerous. Big brother databases jeopardize our national security. The can be exploited to manipulate elections. They can be used to control or harm politicians, news reporters, scientists, accountants, bankers, CEOs, soldiers, and you. Such invasive databases should be illegal. Moreover, *no foreign government or workers should have access to social security numbers and other private information on US citizens.*

Chapter 22

Overwhelming Numbers

The most dangerous is the enemy within.

The amount of foreign travel and foreign trade caused by globalization has grown beyond the means of our government to protect our borders.

A 2002 study reported that *over 500 million people enter our country annually–330 million of these people were not US citizens*. Note: Some people travel frequently, so they would be counted as an entrant each time they enter the US. The number of people in our country that speak foreign languages exploded. The FBI had to hire linguists for Arabic, Farsi, Chinese, and more. Costs for translating recordings increased from $2.5 million in 2001, to $70 million in 2004. That's a 28 fold increase in 3 years! Still the FBI had hundreds of thousands of hours of recordings backlogged. [225]

Annually, our borders were crossed by 11.2 million trucks, and 2.2 million railroad cars, and by sea 7,500 foreign flag ships make 51,000 trips to US ports. [208]

Packages entering the United States from abroad should be checked not only for potential terrorist attack but also for environmental hazards. By *2005, our country had been invaded by 7,000 foreign species that are damaging crops, killing trees, and causing economic losses to the US of $137 billion a year*. And, it could get much worse if an invasive species of plant or animal severely damages our food supply. [530]

Americanizing Overpopulated Countries

Globalization shifts jobs to overpopulated countries where labor is cheaper and easily exploited. This harms nations such as United States that prospered because we controlled our population growth.

Offshoring by US corporations caused our food, gas, and national security costs to soar. *These increased costs more than offset the purported cost savings from globalization for Americans.*

Globalization Siphoning American Jobs & Resources Lowering USA Standard of Living

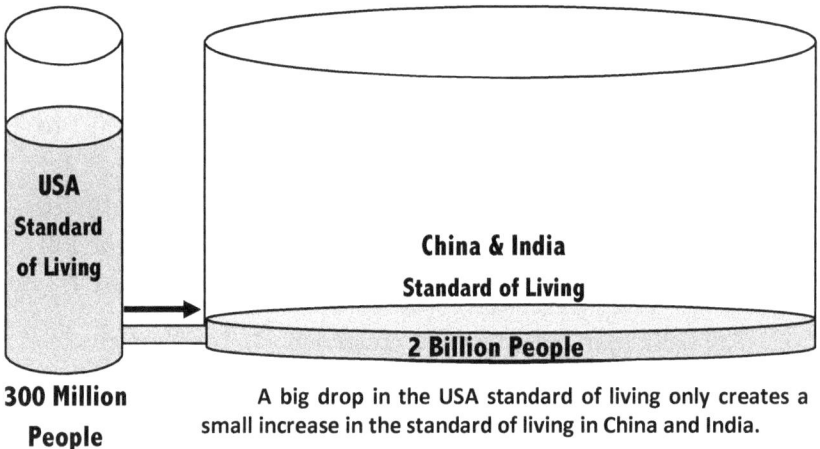

USA Standard of Living

China & India

Standard of Living

2 Billion People

300 Million People

A big drop in the USA standard of living only creates a small increase in the standard of living in China and India.

Moreover, while India and China struggled with overpopulation, we struggled with pollution problems caused by energy consumption and manufacturing. Americanizing overpopulated countries is creating a global environmental catastrophe.

Fake IDs

Because of offshoring foreign nations have the equipment and training to easily produce fake drivers' licenses right down to the holograms and bar codes. According to an April 2012 "License to Terrorize," article on *thedaily.com* terrorists can easily obtain counterfeit IDs online for just $200 that are produced overseas and mailed to the US. These IDs are good enough to fool airport security. Because of these fakes, our government may try to mandate an intrusive national ID that vastly expands government monitoring of US citizens. [1004]

Reduce Travel and Trade

We want to be connected with and trade with nations around the world in a mutually beneficial way. However, it is vital that we reduce and better control the volume of travel and trade. It's like selling tickets to a show, you cannot have people sneaking in from all directions without tickets, and you cannot sell more tickets than you have seats.

Chapter 23

Bioterrorism Risks

How many biological attacks have gone unreported?

Many authorities think we are more at risk from a bioterrorism attack than a nuclear attack. Biological agents can be just as deadly and require less money and skill to use. Because of this threat, since the September 11th attack, our government spending on biological attack defenses increased 18 fold. We are spending over $7 billion per year. [408]

The FDA warned you not to buy medicine online from other countries because medicines sold to Americans could become a target for a biological terrorist attack.

Yet, our government has done little to stop pharmaceutical offshoring. When US pharmaceutical companies offshored production of medicines they enabled sophisticated drug counterfeiting. This gave counterfeiters access to the equipment to make fake drugs that look real down to the stamp on tablets. Only a chemical analysis by the manufacturer can identify if the drug is real.

Drug counterfeiting has gone on for years and is getting worse. For example, in 1998, US Customs seized 2,145 shipments of fake drugs. In 1999, US Customs seized 9,725 shipments. That was a fourfold increase in just one year. [535]

Counterfeit Drugs Injure & Kill

Globalization of our drug industry is dangerous. In 2001, *China and India were identified as the primary global suppliers of the bulk ingredients for fake drugs.* We are purchasing drugs with no assurance that the drugs are safe, potent, or even medicine. [535]

"Tainted Medicine – A Secret Killer" a 2007 article reported corruption in both India and China where some regulators worked *in collusion with the manufactures of counterfeit drugs. Counterfeit drug manufacturers caused mass killings in Nigeria, Argentina, India and Haiti.* [630] The problem is global. For example, it was estimated that 50% of the drugs sold in Pakistan are fake, and 40% of the drugs sold in Nigeria and the Ukraine are fake. [655] A Nigerian pharmacologist called drug counterfeiters mass murders after a batch of toxic medicine killed 100 Nigerian children. [631]

A 2003 *U.S Pharmacist* report, "Counterfeit Drugs A Menace Keeps Growing," warned about the dangers to Americans:

- ■ *"70% to 80% of the key ingredients in American-made generic drugs come from foreign suppliers, as do about 60% of those in their brand name counterparts." Because of the volume, the FDA allows the drugs into our country based on the "representations of an international broker, who could in fact be a counterfeiter." [948]*

- ■ *"Some countries such as Argentina, India, Egypt, and South Africa actually encourage or condone pharmaceutical patent piracy. In India, because patent protection is absent, bulk manufacturers are able to freely pirate the intellectual property of the world's pharmaceutical industry... India drug companies can and do boldly reverse-engineer best-selling drugs such as Viagra, Prozac, Diflucan, Prilosec, and Norvasc." [948]*

In 2006, Dateline TV reported that China, India, Pakistan and other countries were flooding our country with fake drugs. The scope of the counterfeiting and dangers posed to Americans were alarming. [536]

After security costs are factored in, importing "cheaper" drugs may be more costly than producing the drugs in the USA. In 2006, *our government set up a FDA office in China*, the first one outside the US. And, it planned to set up *"two more in China...and ...one in India."* [945] You are being taxed to subsidize offshoring by paying for drug testing in foreign countries.

"Counterfeit Drugs: Infected with Greed," *said counterfeit drug sales in the United States were expected to reach $75 billion in 2010*. Once again China and India were the main source of dangerous fake drugs sold to Americans. [631]

Counterfeit drugs make up a big chunk of our foreign trade deficit. For instance, one US Customs seizure of fake drugs had an estimated market value of $60 million. The trail of these illegal drugs was an indictment against globalization. The captured drugs were produced in India, labeled in California, distributed out of Mexico, and destined for sale to Americans. [535]

China Biological Attacks?

"Chinese pharmaceutical companies have sold fake polio vaccines, blood protein and other drugs." And, Chinese companies *exported poisonous diethylene glycol labeled as a pure sweetener ingredient for cough syrup and food,* according to a 2007 article "In Trade, China's Moral Compass is Off Course." It also claimed that China repackaged and sold expired medicine. And that Chinese companies were using formaldehyde and toxic dyes to make candy, crackers and pickles. Moreover, it claimed China *exported toys coated with lead paint, and put kerosene in toys containing liquid for floating.* [645]

Despite all the corruption, China was supplying 70% of the penicillin, 50% of the aspirin and 35% of the acetaminophen, and many vitamins sold globally. *China makes almost 80% of the toys sold in our country.* The article referred to China as a *"gigantic trillion dollar export machine."* [645]

Another 2007 report, "China Drug Official Given Death Sentence," was an *abcnews.go.com story.* It said a top Chinese drug regulator was caught taking bribes to approve fake drugs. It addressed growing concerns about the safety of Chinese made goods sold to Americans. Our government compiled a list of made in China products suspected of containing dangerous toxins. The list even included juice and toothpaste. [654]

This 'globalization' threat to our medicine supply has gone on for several years. For example, in 1995, fifty tons of toxic counterfeit glycerin was shipped to the US. This US shipment was discovered prior to being distributed in medicine.

However, sometimes deadly foreign drugs are not caught in time.

For example, a 2008 article, "Baxter CEO Tells Congress Heparin Tampering was Deliberate," reported that *"deadly allergic reactions to heparin"* <u>*killed over 80 Americans*</u> and harmed over 1,000 more. It was a "deliberate" biological attack. The tampering was *"so novel and so insidious as to avoid the quality systems of a multitude of companies and the oversight of the world's most sophisticated drug regulatory agencies."* The deadly fake blood-thinner drug was traced to China. Chinese authorities insisted Americans not interfere with their investigation. Because of these deaths, the US Food and Drug Administration (FDA) was criticized for ineffective policies and lack of diligence at the highest levels of its organization. A Chairman of the Congressional panel concluded, *"Our citizens can no longer trust that their food, drugs or medical devices are safe when the FDA says they are."* [691]

The US is China's biggest customer – a dangerous distinction we should quickly rethink.

India and Biological Risks

"India to Introduce Death Penalty for Peddling Fake Drugs," a 2003 article, reported the problem of dangerous fake drugs was severe. The death penalty was proposed for the sellers and distributors of fake drugs if people were severely harmed or killed. As in China, often officials regulating India's drug industry were in collusion with the makers of the fake drugs. [629]

Based on a 2008 *blogs.swj.com/health* article, "Awash in Counterfeit Drugs, India May Pay More For Foreign Approval," it appears that India may be worse than China: "*OECD says 75% of fake drugs around the world have origins in India...*" [715]

In 2009, a *USA Today* article, "FDA Blocks Generic Drug Imports from India," exposed that an India pharmaceutical company was a supplier for "*a U.S. program that funds AIDS drugs for Africa.*" [947] Our taxes were used to buy drugs made in India that were shipped to Africa as foreign aid!

Pandemic Risks

The current level of travel and trade may spread a pandemic too rapidly to give scientists sufficient time to develop a vaccine. And, what if there is a shortage of vaccines during a pandemic and the foreign nation producing our vaccines gets a better offer from another country, or decides that they need the vaccine and refuse to ship us what we need?

Also, what if we depend on another nation for our vaccines and that nation becomes infected with a contagious disease making it unsafe to ship the medicine. Offshoring the production of our vaccines and other medicines poses unacceptable risks.

America needs to manage the development, quality control, and production of our medicines. [454]

Time to Declare War on Autism

One of the worst biological threats to our nation is autism. It has grown to epidemic proportions with 1 in 88 of our children harmed. Strangely, boys are at 4 times the risk as girls.

Autism is worse than polio because it cripples the brain. Have fake drugs or toxic toys or other biological hazards created by outsourcing caused autism? Or, could it be caused by the increase in the number of vaccinations given to our children? Or, is it something in the processing and/or packaging of our food? Is it a combination of factors in our environment? <u>We do not know</u>.

What we do know is that Autism attacks our children. It is heartbreaking for parents to see their children struggle. And, autism jeopardizes our nation's ability to compete globally.

Also consider that our children who do not have autism may be experiencing some brain damage from whatever is causing autism. They may be suffering with other learning difficulties and struggling with social skills. It is time to get some answers. It is time to protect our children.

Stop Outsourcing Drug Production and R&D

No one knows how many Americans have been killed or injured by counterfeit medicines. We need better control of imports to stop this crime. And, we should insist on *a dependable, inexpensive, and quick system for Americans to get medicine tested if they are concerned that it might be counterfeit*.

Offshoring biological research is dangerous. Mishandling of penicillin can create drug resistant superbugs. If safety procedures are not followed researchers may inadvertently release deadly organisms. Biological research should be done by Americans with no monetary conflicts of interest.

Chapter 24

Protecting our Children's

Future

10,000 people could say the dark tis light. Merely one would say it tis night.
Yet, the lonesome one would be right.

A key component of Information Warfare is the psychological attack against a nation. Take away its heroes, take away its victories, take away its belief in itself and you destroy the nation. Our children are being taught diversity and globalization, while children in China and India are being taught that their countries will become the new world powers.

Our media from news to cartoons has been used to promote Asian racial superiority claims to the detriment of non-Asian US children and US workers. They compare science and math scores of students in the US to students from China and India. However, they are not comparing apples to apples. These countries have large numbers of illiterate children who are not included in the tests. As recently as 2006, over 40% of the population in India was illiterate. [513] In contrast, the US tests the majority of our students. Moreover, our test results are skewed downward by massive numbers of students not proficient in English.

It is harmful to our children to have these unfair and contrived comparisons used to support discriminatory educational and job opportunities. [114]

We Need to Take Care of Our Own Children First

For over half a century our foreign aid paid for foreign students to attend our colleges. Instead of returning to their country, students from India and China often stayed here illegally and took jobs. And, even worse they were the hidden drivers behind outsourcing our jobs: "*The pool of people that came to the US and went to school and then ended up often in places like Silicon Valley has paved the way for this outsourcing*." [379]

Yet, a 2006, PBS WideAngle report wanted us to help finance "*a free education to every child in the world by 2015.*" Anchor Daljit Dhaliwal asked, "*was the United States leading the challenge on global education?*" Gene Sperling from the Council on Foreign Relations said we should spend $2.5 to 3 billion to *win hearts and minds* to become "*the champions of global education.*" [541] The goal was to *pay for the education of 100 million children in countries such as Africa and India.* The US was described as a rich nation not putting in our share. [541] *Have they looked at our trade deficit? We need to focus on educating our own children. Their future is in great jeopardy.*

Have we won hearts and minds? Call center workers in India said talking with an American is "*like talking to a child,*" in a 2006 *ABC News* story: "*India Inc.-Call Centers, Surgeons, Tutors Serve Americas.*" They said it is a "*common practice*" to put Americans on hold while they curse at them. A tutor in India *said that a 10th grader in the US would be on the level of a 7th grader in India.* Even worse they claimed that a "*35-year-old American's IQ is the same as a 10-year-old Indian's IQ.*" [501] News anchors failed to challenge this nonsense.

- *The Intelligence Quotient = (Mental Age/Chronological Age)* 100. So if an Indian at 10 has the mental age of a 35 year old American then (35/10)* 100 = IQ of 350, which is not credible.*

- *Or if a 35 year old American has the IQ of a 10 year old which would be calculated as (10/35)*100 = an IQ of 29, again not credible.*

We Even Educated & Employed Terrorists

The *Times Square bomb prime suspect, Pakistani Faisal Shahzad entered our country on a student visa.* Like millions of other foreign students he then got an *H-1B visa.* He married *"an apparent US citizen,"* who helped him get a green card, and then US citizenship. "Bomb Suspect's Citizenship Raises Questions About Naturalization Process," was a 2010 *Fox News* report. It exposed that student visas, H-1B visas, green cards and citizenship had been granted to *terrorist suspects "implicated in terror plots inside the United States."* [1012]

Also, consider that 15 of the 19 September 11th terrorists were Saudis. Yet *rawstory.com* in 2010 reported that "Kagan Helped Shield Saudis from 9/11 Lawsuits." [1013] *These terrorists were educated in Saudi schools and Mosques.* How many schools and Mosques have Saudis been allowed to build in the US? MSNBC's 2011 story, "Islamic Schools on the Rise in US, Look for Acceptance." [1014]

College Acceptance Rates

Spin doctors from India claimed, *"it is safe to assume"* that India's IIT graduates are as good or better than Harvard graduates because the admission rate for IIT's was 2.2% while for Harvard it was 12.5%. [30] These rates have more to do with population density per university opportunity than quality of education. There is no empirical evidence demonstrating that overpopulation increases the quality of education. In fact due to the strains of on limited educational resources it is more likely that overpopulation lowers the quality of education. This may explain India's high illiteracy rate.

Significantly, they admitted that IIT graduates had to *"do a mandatory two-year stint at a US university"* before they could get a job in Silicon Valley. [30] This would debunk superiority claims. *And it exposes there was never a need for US companies to hire H-1Bs. Moreover, students get non-immigrant visas so it was illegal to stay here on these visas.*

Demand a Demographic Discrimination Audit

Vinod Khosla, an immigrant from India, in a 60 Minutes interview said *that in Silicon Valley H-1B job applicants from India "are favored over almost anybody else."* He even said: *"If you are a WASP (White Anglo-Saxon Protestant) walking in for a job, you wouldn't have as much pre-assigned credibility as you do if you're an engineer from the Indian Institute of Technology."* [323] *They discriminated against Americans when hiring in America!*

It is time to demand demographic audits of college professors and students at our universities to see if they mirror our population or if WASPs are being discriminated against in educational opportunities and financial aid. It is also time to demand a demographic audit of our government research contract awards and government labs. What percentage of our government defense research has been and is being done by non-Americans? It is time to do an audit of our high tech and other jobs to see if WASPs are fairly represented.

"21 and the World is Yours"

A 2008, *ABC News* series "21 and the World is Yours," featured 21 year olds in China, India, Egypt, and Kenya.

The show for India said they searched for *"a compelling 21-year old in Mumbia,"* and selected a Sales Manager for a Medical Testing Company. They described her in glowing terms such as *"regal bearing," "gale-force smile."* She was living at home with her parents and insisted that she would not marry outside her community (*caste?*). There was even a portion of the report "America Not as Cool as We Think?" [683]

Contrast this to how young white women are sexualized in the media. A working 21 year old white girl living at home with her parents waiting for a love match exclusive to her community to get married would be ridiculed.

21 and is Any Place in the World is Yours?

Do Baby Boomers' children and grandchildren have a future? "Whites Account for Under Half of Births in US," a May 2012 article in *The New York Times* reported. "*This is an important tipping point... from a mostly white baby boomer culture to the more globalized multiethnic country that we are becoming.*" said Brookings Institution demographer William H. Frey. The article celebrated "*a milestone for a nation whose government was founded by white Europeans.*" [1010]

The article said this was a "*highly charged*" because of immigration. [1010] It failed to address how this change was brought about by political deceit, visa fraud, and illegal immigration.

■ *When Americans objected to the 1965 Immigration Act–Senator Edward Kennedy promised: "First, our cities will not be flooded with a million immigrants annually. Under the proposed bill, the present level of immigration remains substantially the same...Secondly, the ethnic mix of this country will not be upset..." [994] Both not true.*

Dowell Myers a University of Southern California professor said "*If the US depended on white births alone, we'd be dead.*" [1010] *If it is a "globalized" trend where are the reciprocal white births in China, India, the Middle East, and Mexico? Why the decline in white births?*

■ *Losing jobs and health insurance to H-1Bs impacted marriage rates broke apart families and in turn caused lower white birthrates.*

■ *Statistics show 50% to 75% of Americans graduating from college cannot find jobs. And, even if they find jobs many cannot afford to have a child because they owe tens of thousands in college loan debt.*

■ *An unfair number, about 75%, of our soldiers killed in the current war were white. Plus, many surviving soldiers have injuries that impact fertility. What ethnic groups fail to carry their fair share?*

The media claimed "*educating young minorities was of critical importance to the future of the country and the economy.*" [994] It is a cycle. Discrimination caused reduced white birth rates, which in turn was used to argue for more discrimination.

A Future for Our Children

H-1B visas and offshoring are devastating baby boomers children. Layoffs shattered families. Young school age children could hardly be expected to do well in school when their world is falling apart. A despondent unemployed parent may not be able to help with homework while they are worried about losing their home. Many bright high school students lost their hope of going to college when their parents lost their job. Young Americans graduating from college were disheartened and discouraged when they invested in a college education and could not get a job.

The H-1B visas unfairly pitted 22 year old American college graduates against 27-30 year old foreign students graduating with masters and doctoral degrees for entry level jobs in our country. Foreigners even got minority benefits. Ironically we funded their education to win hearts and minds. Why were our politicians so callous and uncaring about the hearts and minds of young Americans? A whole generation of Americans is being denied their inheritance and a chance at the American Dream.

An astounding 40 million naturalized citizens now live in our country. Many came here on non-immigrant visas. We have naturalized people whose allegiance is to a foreign country, not the US. We have naturalized terrorists.

Obama's Administration was altering the demographics of our population for ages 30 and younger with an amnesty, "rubberstamping" student and H-1B visas and giving out green cards. [901] Our government with its lax immigration policies granted citizenship to people who hate our country and our culture. Are our colleges even teaching Western Civilization anymore? Our children have a right to celebrate their history and to a bright future.

Chapter 25

Restore our National Security

"These are the times that try men's souls. The summer soldier and the sunshine patriot will, in this crisis, shrink from the service of their country; but he that stands it now, deserves the love and thanks of man and woman. Tyranny, like hell, is not easily conquered; yet we have this consolation with us, that the harder the conflict, the more glorious the triumph. –Thomas Payne

When you look at how our country's computer networks, telecom companies, and research labs have been penetrated by "countries of concern" *there is probably no secure area that has not been compromised*. Cyber attacks on our computers are growing. Foreign programmers have gained access to strategic computer systems. In some cases they were foolishly put in charge of system security. Our *"tech-illiterate leadership in Washington,"* has put us in real and present danger. [226]

Biological threats loom large. Offshoring has our pharmaceutical industry plagued with foreign counterfeit drugs.

Our goal is to sever from our nation the enemy within. It is not enough to cut a weed, it must be pulled out from the roots, or it will just sprout again. The root of this problem is lax and excessive student visa allotments used by foreign governments for outsourcing, spying and technology theft.

Only Americans with undivided loyalty to the US should do our defense R&D, and manage the IT systems that control our weapons, our financial transactions, our elections, our medical records, our power grid, and more.

Ending the Trade Deficit is Essential to Security

Our trade deficit is dangerous. It strikes at the foundation of our national security. How can we use trade sanctions to resolve conflicts when we are the biggest debtor nation in the world? A strategic transition plan is needed to rebuild our prosperity. Tax incentives to offshore need to be replaced by tax incentives to build up American businesses and hire Americans. Targeted tariffs are also needed to protect surviving US businesses. And to bring industry back, progressive tariffs strategy could help rebuild.

Some people say we shouldn't worry because the trade deficit is not debt we have to repay. Yes, the trade deficit is not loans. It is worse–they hold our *money, US Treasury bonds, US corporations, and other US assets.* We need an honest and fair audit so that we settle our obligations and regain ownership *of foreign holdings of US Treasury bonds and other US assets.* Such an audit may find that they actually owe us money.

There is a legal term called "clean hands doctrine." This doctrine requires that the party making a claim must not have done anything unfair or wrong to create the financial obligation. If the claimant misled the defendant or did something wrong they have "unclean hands" related to their claims and they can be denied their judgment. [624]

Espionage and reverse engineering and selling counterfeits would break this "clean hands" requirement. As would bribing US executives and US politicians and luring them with fraudulent university "studies" to profit from visas and offshoring. And what about the billions US corporations were lured to spend to build research labs and corporate campuses in these countries? China and India also need to pay us for patent and copyright infringements, counterfeiting, and other unjust gain.

We Need to Reverse Globalization

Globalization set the stage for global economic collapse because of the excessive amount of entangling of economies. There's an old saying "don't put all your eggs in one basket." If everything is in one basket and the basket falls everything breaks.

Terrorists organize into cells, so that if one cell is destroyed the other cells continue. Our leaders should understand this simple concept. As much as possible, each nation's economy should be structured to stand alone. Economies should be enhanced by global trade but not dependent on it to survive.

People in Other Nations Harmed

China and India are not developing nations. These are nations with a long history of civilization and culture.

Globalization not only harms Americans. It harms people subjected to oppressive foreign governments. For example, the Chinese government used search engine technology provided by American companies to censor pro-democracy data, expand surveillance, and track private communications of its citizens. [157] [533] [580] Also, polluted air and water caused by globalization created major health and economic problems for many Chinese people. Pollution killed crops and fouled the air and water. Factories were built in poor agricultural areas where land was cheap. The problem–this cheap land was all that many families had. When families dependent on the land for their living protested they risked governmental retaliation and arrest. [582]

If we claim to be a nation that promotes freedom, we should not be helping foreign governments oppress their people.

It's Time for Some Common Sense

Our country is in grave danger on many sides from cyber attacks, to financial attacks, to biological attacks, to cultural attacks. It is time to be less "politically correct," and more common sense correct.

How foolish is it to pay for commercial and military research done by foreign students, especially students that come from "countries of concern."

The size and scope of how outsourcing has jeopardized our national security is vast.

We are dependent on our government to *protect* our national interests. Our media has been manipulated to make the word protectionist a bad thing. Common sense would dictate that a level of protection is essential to survival. George Washington believed that trade laws should be structured to *protect* the vital interests of the United States. Trade laws were supposed to *protect* our nation's industrial base, independence, and the power of the republic. [231] For seventy years the Republican Party proclaimed to be protectionist on its party platform. It was during this period that we became the world's greatest industrial power.

We are in a very vulnerable situation. Think of those action movies where a major catastrophe is rapidly approaching and just in the nick of time they save the world. Like our forefathers we need to kneel down and pray for our nation, and then we need to stand up united together. The land of the free only belongs to the brave. What we are facing is very serious and we need to act wisely and quickly.

Bibliography

Referenced sources are arranged in numeric order according to the reference numbers located in [brackets] in the document text. This book is the culmination of extensive research; only sources referenced in this book are included in this bibliography. Therefore, you will see breaks in the number sequence such as: reference number "6" followed by reference number "8", because reference number "7" in the complete documents list was not used in this book.

Note: Web addresses do not include the www prefix, and only contain the first part of the path. This address information or a search engine query for the title should be sufficient to help locate the articles and websites. Note also that some articles may have been removed, and some websites may have been changed from the time the research was done.

1: Rupert Cornwell, *Interview: Professor JK Galbraith*, The Independent, 7/1/2002.

6: Sarah Anderson, John Cavanagh, Chris Hartman, Scott Klinger, and Stacy Chan, *Executive Excess 2004 Campaign Contributions, Outsourcing, Unexpensed Stock Options and Rising CEO Pay*, Institute for Policy Studies and United for a Fair Economy, 8/31/2004.

23: Peter Schrag, *Feinstein's Rule*, prospect.org, 12/17/2001.

29: Rep. Tom Tancredo, *H-1B Visas -- A Time to Cut Back*, h1bprotest.com, 12/30/2002.

30: Pradipta Bagchi, *Visas for business or bondage?*, y-axix.com, 7/6/2000.

38: Charles J. Murray, *Engineer Shortage Called Danger to Military Readiness*, EE Times/ programmersguild.org, 9/21/2000.

43: Rob Sanchez, *H-1B Newsletter Get the Facts on H-1B*, zazona.com, 6/28/2002.

45: Ed Frauenheim, *Scourge of Silicon Valley --5*, salon.com, 10/19/2000.

47: Dr. Gene A. Nelson, *A Brief History of H-1B*, zazona.com, 5/4/2001.

53: Preston Gralla, *Worker Visas Under Fire*, cio.com, 1/15/2002.

59: *Demographics of the Typical H-1B*, zazona.com, Web Date 24-Apr-01.

63: Phyllis Schlafly Report, *What the Global Economy Costs Americans*, eagleforum.org, 6/3/2003.

67: Winston Chai, CNETAsia, *India: IT Outsourcing Aids U.S. Other Economies*, asia.cnet.com, 7/14/2003.

73: *Hard Times in Silicon Valley*, cbsnews.com, 7/14/2003.

75: Jim Ericson, *The Offshore Value Chain*, line56.com, 3/27/2003.

76: John Ribeiro, InfoWorld, *BPO bound for Bombay*, indusdemographics.com, 3/22/2002.

77: *Information Technology Enabled Services*, offshoreis.com, Web Date 16-Nov-02.

78: Gislen Software, *Making the Choice and making IT Work!*, gseindia.com, Web Date 11-Feb-02.

80: RTTS Services - Outsourcing Statistics, *Statistic Related to Offshore Outsourcing*, rttsweb.com, 5/27/2005.

81: Paul Craig Roberts, *Outsourcing: A Greater Threat Than Terrorism*, newsmax.com, 4/22/2005.

85: Rick Wray, *"India's Tech Firms braced for U.S. Fallout"*, thestandard.com, 3/14/2001.

88: Board of Directors, *IEEE USA: Position Offshore Outsourcing*, ieeeusa.org, 3/1/2004.

89: Anupama Chandrasekaran, *Silence is Golden for Outsourcing*, ciol.com, 4/27/2004.

90: *Outsourcing to India*, gnp.org/india, Web Date 31-Mar-03.

92: Pradeep Kurup, *Data Security Trips Indian BPO*, economictimes.indiatimes.com, 4/29/2004.

93: Pragati Verma and Puja Mehra, *US Companies may have to reveal details of offshore deals*, economictimes.indiatimes.com, 4/13/2004.

94: The Economic Times Online, *Frauds be Damned, BPO biz grows*, economictimes.indiatimes.com, 7/7/2005.

100: David Zielenziger, Reuters, *Corrected - US Companies Quietly Moving More Jobs Overseas*, money.excite.com, 12/24/2003.

101: Hughes Software Systems, *Area Companies Reaping Benefits of Outsourcing*, hssworld.com, 6/28/2001.

105: Jennifer Bjorhus, San Joes Mercury News, *USA: Slowdown Sending Tech Jobs Overseas*, corpwatch.org, 10/21/2002.

107: Reuters, *Report: 1 in 10 Tech Jobs May Move Offshore*, news.cxcite.com, 7/29/2003.

110: CET Archives, *Enron, India, and Globalization*, cin.org, 2/4/2002.

112: Rosemary Arakaparambil, *U.S. Firms Eye More Outsourcing to India*, Reuters, 6/26/2003.

114: Technology News, *Tech Firms Defend Moving Jobs Overseas*, start.earthlink.net, 1/7/2004.

116: Bill Moyers, *America and Jobs*, pbs.org, 11/7/2004.

117: The Hindu Business Line, *Sun Grows 70 pc, Expands India Presence*, blonnet.com, 6/29/2000.

121: Rashmi Sharma Singh, *H Workers in Limbo*, indolink.com, 1/30/2001.

122: Terry Atlas, *Bangalore's Big Dreams*, U.S. News & World Report, 5/2/2005.

123: K.C. Krishnadas, *India's Tech Industry Defends H-1B, Outsource Roles*, Electronic Engineering Times.com, 7/10/2003.

124: India Business Opportunities, *Electronics & Information Technology*, ficci.com/ficci/india-profile, Web Date 4-Nov-02.

128: *Regional Advantage Notes - ITEC 1210 (IT Revolution)*, greenvertigo.net, 11/1/2001.

130: Mike Lee, *Long-Distance Service*, abcnews.go.com, 2/15/2002.

133: Michael Fitzgerald, freelance writer, *Big Savings Big Risk*, csoonline.com, 11/1/2003.

135: Christopher H. Schmitt, *Wages of Sin - Why Lawbreakers still win government contracts*, U.S. News & World Report, 5/13/2002.

139: Tim Weiner and James Risen, New York Times, *Policy Makers, Diplomats, Intelligence Officers All Missed India's Intentions*, mtholyoke.edu, 5/25/1998.

141: *Shipping Jobs Overseas: How Real is the Problem*, aflcio.org, Web Date 27-May-05.

146: Paul McDougall, InformationWeek, *Outsourcing Overseas Brings Consumer Privacy Concerns*, securitypipeline.com, 3/15/2004.

148: Tim Whitmire, Associated Press Writer, *Wachovia in bind Over Bank Acquisition*, boston.com, 6/30/2005.

149: Paul Nowell, Associated Press, *BofA Consuming MBNA*, newsobserver.com, 7/2/2005.

150: Eric Dash, *Lost Credit Data Improperly Kept, Company Admits*, nytimes.com, 6/20/2005.

152: Associated Press, *Bush Signs Identity Theft sentencing Law*, earthlink.net, 7/15/2004.

157: Associated Press, *China Extends Text Message Surveillance*, earthlink.net, 7/2/2004.

159: Robert O'Harrow Jr., staff writer, *Bahamas Firm Screens Personal Data to Assess Risk*, washingtonpost.com, 10/16/2004.

160: Warren E. Buffett and Carol J. Loomis, *America's Growing Trade Deficit is Selling The Nation Out From Under Us. Here's a Way to Fix the Problem -- And We Need to Do It Now*, Fortune, 11/10/2003.

161: Embassy of India, *India's Information Technology Industry*, indianembassy.org, Web Date 27-May-05.

162: Dawn Kawamoto, *Oracle Buys PeopleSoft for $10 Billion*, news.com.com, 12/13/2004.

163: Gareth Morgan, *The PeopleSoft dilemma: skip battle or face cull?*, infoconomy.com, 1/1/2005.

164: Justice Litle, *China's Hunger for Knowledge*, dailyreckoning.com, Web Date 8-Mar-05.

165: George Leopold, *With Eye On China, DoD Task Force Warns of IC Drain*, EE Times Online, 4/25/2005.

166: Cliff Edwards, AP Technology Writer, *High-Tech World Has Low-Tech Spying*, new.excite.com, 6/30/2000.

167: Paul Craig Roberts, *Is Outsourcing Trade - Or Dispossession?*, stoptheinvasion.com, 3/4/2003.

168: Associated Press, *China Studying U.S. Complaint to WTO*, earthlink.net, 3/19/2004.

170: Albert H. Teich, *R&D in the Federal Budget: Frequently Asked Questions*, aaas.org, Web Date 23-Aug-05.

171: Data Brief National Science Foundation, *R&D Spending is Highly Concentrated in a Small Number of States*, nsf.gov, 3/23/2001.

172: Gilbert M. Gaul and Susan Q Stranahan, Inquirer Staff Writers and Frank Donahue, *How Billions in Taxes Failed to Create Jobs*, corporations.org, 6/4/1995.

173: The McAlvany Intelligence Advisor, *Red Tide: The Chinese Communist Targeting of America*, special-guests.com, 5/1/1997.

176: U.S. Commercial Service India, *Computer and Software Services*, buyusa.gov, 11/6/2002.

177: Associated Press, *U.S. Trade Deficit Hits Record in 2003*, earthlink.net, 2/13/2004.

179: Associated Press, *Greenspan: China Revaluation Won't Help*, bellsouth.net, 5/22/2005.

180: BBC News, *China Oil Firm in Unocal Bid War*, newsvote.bbc.co.uk, 6/23/2005.

181: Becca Mader, *How Much Government is Too Much?*, milwaukee.bizjournals.com, 7/16/2004.

182: Nasscom, *Software Piracy Statistics*, nasscom.org, Web Date 11-Feb-02.

183: Paul Nowell, Associated Press, *Analysts divided on $3B BoA Investment*, boston.com, 6/18/2005.

184: Mary Mosquera, *TechNet Targets Permanent R&D Tax Credit*, techweb.com, 2/24/1999.

185: Nancy Forbes, *Federal Programs Link Industry and Academia*, American Institute of Physics, 4/1/1999.

193: Bara Vaida, National Journal's Technology Daily, *Cybersecurity Czar Meets with Tech Execs*, govexec.com, 11/8/2001.

199: Wes Vernon, *China's Huge Spy Network in U.S.*, freerepublic.com, 3/15/2005.

200: Don O'Neill, Global Software Competitiveness Studies, *Competitiveness, Security, and the Law*, members.aol.com, 11/1/2002.

201: Steve Ranger, *Security Worries Hit Offshore Outsourcing*, management.silicon.com, 4/26/2005.

202: Harris Corporation, *Computer Security Facts and Statistics from Harris Corporation*, bigwave.ca, Web Date 7-Mar-02.

203: Fragomen, Del Rey, Bernsen & Loewy P.C., *US Immigration Headlines: DOD to Curb Computer Access by Foreign Nationals*, pubweb.fdbl.com, 3/8/2002.

204: *Bennett Applauds Bush Appointment of Cybersecurity Advisor*, senate.gov, 10/9/2001.

205: Eric Chabrow, *IT Innovation Drives Homeland-Security Efforts*, informationweek.com, 2/25/2002.

206: Hindustant Times Correspondent, *Hackers Giving CIA a Tough Time*, hindustantimes.com, 6/25/2001.

207: Eric Chabrow, *Mild-Mannered IT Champion: Tom Ridge*, informationweek.com, 10/8/2001.

208: President George W. Bush, *Securing the Homeland Strengthening the Nation*, whitehouse.gov/homeland, 3/5/2002.

209: Condikeezza Rice and Tom Ridge, *New Counter-Terrorism and CyberSpace Security Positions Announced*, whitehouse.gov, 10/9/2001.

211: D. Ian Hopper, *House Passes Computer Security Bill*, apnews.excite.com, 2/7/2002.

213: Andrew Robinson, *Why U.S. Hands are Tied as India Readies New Missile Tests*, pacificnews.org/jinn, 1/25/1999.

216: Victoria Ward, *Briton Guilty in Arms Deal Trap Set Up by FBI Sting*, scotsman.com, 4/28/2005.

217: Amy Klein, Staff Writer, *Missile Seller Guilty of Aiding Terrorism*, northjersey.com, 4/28/2005.

218: Nabanita Sircar, *Brit-Indian Admits Laundering $86,000 for Hemant Lakhani*, hindustantimes.com, 9/11/2005.

222: Ted Bridis, Associated Press, *Tech Firms: We Must Export Jobs*, cbsnews.com, 1/7/2004.

224: Hearing of the Immigration and Claims Subcommittee, *Oral Testimony of Gene A,. Nelson, Ph.D. Regarding U.S. High Tech Workforce*, zazona.com, 8/5/1999.

225: Curt Anderson, Associated Press, *FBI Far Behind Translating Spy Tapes*, The News and Observer, 9/28/2004.

226: David Kirkpatrick, Fortune.com, *Will the U.S. Fall Behind in Tech?*, cnn.com, 10/23/2002.

228: Ashank Desai, *Making of a Software Superpower*, timescomputing.com, 3/31/1999.

230: George J. Borjas, National Review, *Rethinking Foreign Students: A Question of National Interest*, ksghome.harvard.edu, 6/17/2002.

231: Patrick J. Buchanan, *Trading Seabiscuit for a Rabbit*, worldnetdaily.com, 8/4/2003.

233: Irene Brown, *Let's Do Launch*, Popular Science, 8/1/2002.

240: Des Dearlove and Stuart Crainer, The Conference Board, *The Indians Are Coming, How Management Thinkers From India are Changing the Face of American Business*, conference-board.org, 7/1/2005.

241: The Economic Times Online, *US, India tie up to Provide e-learning*, economictimes.indiatimes.com, 7/23/2005.

244: Chidanand Rajghatta, *Wireless Whisper: Design Network Begins to Takeover Telecom World*, indianexpress.com, 7/13/2000.

246: Michael Dorgan, *Chinese Families Pay Big Money for U.S. Student Visas*, americanvisas.com, 4/2/2000.

247: Geoff Brumfiel, *US Universities Up in Arms Over License Plans for Foreign Staff*, nature.com, 10/6/2004.

249: National Science Foundation, *Foreign Doctoral Recipients with plans to Stay in the United States*, nsf.gov, Web Date 27-Feb-05.

252: Federation for American Immigration Reform, *Foreign Students in the United States*, fairus.org, 11/4/2004.

253: Tom Walsh, *University of Michigan Center in India Aims to Help U.S.*, thebatt.com, 5/19/2004.

262: Leslie D'Monte, *MIT Media Lab in India*, zdnetindia.com, 2/15/2001.

271: The Daily Reckoning, *Rude Awakening*, dailyreckoning.com, 5/27/2005.

272: Numbers USA, *Did Congress Intend a huge Increase in Numbers after 1965?*, numbersusa.com/overpopulation, Web Date 27-Feb-05.

275: John H. Tanton, *Commons Sense on Mass Immigration*, commonsenseonmassimmigration.us, 2/1/2004.

278: Charles R. Smith, *Clinton-Approved Computer Exports Help China Build Atomic Bombs*, newsmax.com, 10/4/2002.

279: Kenneth R. Timmerman, *Has Clinton's China Policy Put U.S. National Security at Risk?*, insightmag.com, 2003.

295: *The Dot-Com Crash: March 11, 2000 to October 9, 2002*, investopedia.com, Web Date 13-Jul-05.

300: Manjeet Kripalani and Pete Engardio, *The Rise of India*, BusinessWeek, 12/8/2003.

301: Mike Yamamoto, staff writer Cnet News.com, *Will India Price Itself out of the Offshore Market?*, freeborders.com, 3/29/2004.

303: Manjeet Kripalani in Bombay, with Pete Engardia and Leah Nathans Spiro in New York, *India's WHIZ KIDS (int'l edition), Inside the Indian Institutes of Technology's Star Factory*, businessweek.com/1998/49/b3607011.htm, 11/25/1998.

307: IndiaExpress Bureau, *Lack of Talent, Low Cost Make Outsourcing Inevitable for US*, indiaexpress.com, 12/23/2003.

308: CBS Worldwide Inc., *Out of India*, cbsnews.com, 1/11/2004.

310: *TiE-Rockies Speakers 2000-2001*, tie-rockies.org, Web Date 14-May-02.

313: A P Kamath in Santa Clara, *Plotting Tech Battles for the 21st Century*, rediff.com, 9/16/1999.

318: Indo-Asian News Service, New Jersey, *Gujarat Promotes State as Outsourcing Destination*, indiaday.org, 11/24/2003.

323: Lesly Stahl, *Imported from India*, 60 Minutes, 3/2/2003.

330: Chidanand Rajghatta, *Where Integrated Chip means Indians, Chinese*, indian-express.com, 2/23/2000.

334: Vishwas Varghese, *Information Superpower India?*, swordoftruth.com, 5/20/2000.

335: Y--Axis: Recruit from India, *The Indian Software Industry*, y-axis.com, Web Date 4-Nov-02.

352: *About USAID in India History*, usaid.gov, 4/4/2003.

353: Brett D Schaefer, *Does U.S. Foreign Assistance Elicit Support for U.S. Policy? Not at the United Nations*, heritage.org, 10/22/1999.

355: William K Tabb, *New Economy ?Same Irrational Economy*, monthlyreview.org, 4/2/2001.

368: Non-Resident Indians, *Govt Sets up NRI Group on IT*, welcome-nri.com, 1/2/2000.

372: AnnaLee Saxenian, *Silicon Valley's New Immigrant Entrepreneurs*, The Center for Comparative Immigration Studies, University of California, San Diego, 5/1/2000.

378: Shyamanuja Das and Ch Srinivas Rao, *Tech Start-ups: Indus Valley, Circa 2002*, CIOL Cybertimes, voicendata.com, 9/7/2002.

379: NPR-- All Things Considered, Outsourcing entrepreneurs going back home to export American jobs, *neoIT-Atul Vashistha Discusses Outsourcing*, neoit.com, 3/16/2004.

380: Nina Mehta, New Delhi, *BSA initiates action to check software piracy*, hindustantimes.com, 5/8/2001.

391: Dr. G. Singh, *The Post-1947 Brahmanist Order and its Ideological Foundation*, 1997.

398: Michael Lehman President Flinchbaugh Engineering, York Pa., *Line Transfer: An Alternative to Offshore Manufacturing*, Machine Design, 10/7/2004.

402: Brian Bergstein AP Technology Writer, *Panel Seeks Protections from Data Mining*, zwire.com, 6/26/2004.

405: Chindand Rajghatta, Times of India, *2020 AD: India may Outshine US*, timesofindia.intiatimes.com, 1/14/2005.

406: Ted Hoff Biography, *Important Historical Inventions and Inventors*, ideafinder.com, Web Date 13-Oct-05.

407: Richard McCormack, *Political Appointees Re-Write Commerce Department Report on Offshore Outsourcing; Original Analysis is Missing from Final Version*, manufacturingnews.com, 10/12/2005.

408: Charles J. Hanley AP Special Correspondent, *Can Billions of Dollars Build Biodefenses?*, abcnews.go.com/International, Web Date 16-Mar-06.

409: Eugene J. Huang, Virginia Secretary of Technology, *COVITS 2005 The Promise of Digital Government*, COVITS 2005 Office, Vienna VA, 9/19/2005.

412: Amendments to the Constitution, *The Bill of Rights*, usinfo.state.gov, Web Date 5-Oct-05.

419: The Global Information Society Project Program on Information and Warfare, *Program on Information and Warfare*, information-warfare.info/, 4/1/2005.

420: Bruce Berkowitz, *Warfare in the Information Age*, ndu.edu/inss/books/Books%20-%201998/Inforamtion%20Age%20 Anthology?, 1995.

422: *Interview of Prime Minister Dr. Manhohan Singh on Charlie Rose Show*, indianembassy.org/pm/pm Charlie rose sep 21 04.htm, 9/21/2004.

425: IACPA, *Indian American Center for Political Awareness*, iacfpa.org, Web Date 5-Nov-05.

427: Beth Fouhy, The Associated Press, *Schwarzenegger Kicks Off Far East Tour*, seattletimes.newsource.com, 11/15/2005.

428: Congressman Sanders, *We Must End our Disastrous Trade Policy with China*, bernie.house.gov, 4/14/2005.

429: Matt Moore, Associate Press, *Nations Urge U.S. to Cede Internet Control*, abcnews.go.com, 2006.

430: Mike Moffatt, *American-Japanese Trade and Exchange Analysis*, economics.about.com, 2005.

434: D. Ian Hopper, *CIA Can't Foresee Computer Attacks, Official Says*, Associated Press, 6/21/2001.

435: William Jackson, GCN Staff, *U.S. is Losing Ground on IT Security, Witnesses Tell Hill*, Post-Newsweek Media, Inc, 7/2/2001.

442: The Center for Public Integrity, *Outsourcing the Pentagon*, publicintegrity.org, 9/29/2004.

445: National Intelligence Council's 2020 Project, *Mapping the Global Future: The 2020 Global Landscape*, cia.gov/nic, Web Date 21-Nov-05.

447: Nicholas Makhoff, *Confab: Chips, China Good Investments*, Electronic Engineering Times, 1/16/2006.

448: Mike Clendenin, *China Question Dogs Taiwan's IC Industry*, Electronic Engineering Times, 1/16/2006.

449: Yahoo Finance, *Comtech Group, Inc. to Present at Needham & Company, LLC Growth Conference*, biz.yahoo.com/prnews, 12/30/2005.

452: David Roman, *Dispiriting Days for EEs*, Electronic Engineering Times, 11/14/2005.

454: John L. Helgerson, Chairman, National Intelligence Cou8ncil, *The National Security Implications of Global Demographic Change*, cia.gov/nic/speeches, 4/30/2002.

466: CMP Worldwide Media Networks, *One Stop Media Buying Source for Global Marketers*, cmpworldwide.com/, 2/14/2006.

470: Eric Pfanner and Heather Timmons, *Buyout Bid for Parent of Nielsen*, nytimes.com/2006/01/17/business, 1/17/2006.

472: Associated Press, NSNBC.com, *VNU Receives Buyout Offer from Investor Group*, msnbc.msn.com/id/, 1/16/2006.

474: Tianjin Economic-Technological Development Area, *China IC Maker Ramps*, Electronic Engineering Times, 11/7/2005.

475: Tom Espiner, *Security Experts Lift Lid on Chinese Hack Attacks*, CNET News.com, 11/23/2005.

477: Anthony Kujawa, Washington File Staff Writer, *Foreign Student Enrollment at U.S. Graduate Schools Up in 2005*, usinfo.state.gov, 11/7/2005.

479: Daniel Brook, *Are Your Lawyers in New York or New Delhi?*, legalaffairs.org, 6/1/2005.

480: Patrick Honsson, Christian Science Monitor, *Offshoring Bank Jobs A Records Risk?*, cbsnews.com/stories/2006/01/06/business, 1/6/2006.

484: Michael Fitzgerald, *Is U.S. Losing the Innovation Arms Race*, cioinsight.com, 6/5/2005.

485: *Innovation Takes More Than Just Ambition*, cioinsight.com, 6/5/2005.

488: Edwin S. Rubenstein, The Hudson Institute, *Trade Drag?*, americanoutlook.org, 6/1/2001.

490: Associated Press, *America's Trade Deficit Hits All-Time High*, , Web Date 10-Feb-06.

493: Mathew Fordahy, AP Technology Writer, *Group Sues AT&T Over Alleged Surveillance*, seattlepi.nwsource.com, 1/31/2006.

495: Weiss Research, Inc., *Housing Bust Spreading!*, 11/21/2005.

497: Simon Romero and Heather Timmons, New York Times, *Foreign Management of U.S. Ports Nothing New*, azcentral.com, 2/25/2006.

498: Ophir Falk and Yaron Schwartz, ICT Associate, *Terror at Sea The Maritime Threat*, ict.org.il, 4/25/2005.

499: USA Today, *Foreign Investment Affects Americans' Lives Every Day*, usatoday.com, 2/22/2006.

500: Ashok Sharma, Associated Press Writer, *India Protests U.S. Nuke Statement*, interestalert.com, Web Date 1-Mar-06.

501: ABC News, *India Inc. -- Call Centers, Surgeons, Tutors Serve Americans*, abcnews.go.com/Business, 3/2/2006.

506: Indrajit Basu, *India IT Manufacturing Takes Off*, atimes.com, 3/8/2006.

511: Patrick J. Buchanan, *Free-Trade Policy Hurts U.S. in Bush Era*, mercurynews.com, 2/15/2006.

512: S.L. Bachman, Pacific Council on International Policy, The Western Partner of the Council on Foreign Relations, *Globalization in the San Francisco Bay Area: Trying to Stay at the Head of the Class*, 1/2/2003.

513: ABC News Internet Ventures, *A Billion Reasons to Care About India -- India is a Global Force to Be Reckoned With-- Its Economy is Booming*, abcnews.go.com/GMA, 3/1/2006.

522: Mike Clendenin, *China's First CPU Maker Shifts Gears to Survive*, Electronic Engineering Times, 4/25/2005.

523: multiple authors, *Technology Without Borders Global iit2005 Conference*, iit2005.org, 2005.

530: Earl Swift, *Can They Be Stopped?*, Parade, 5/22/2005.

532: Dr. Jonathan Fink, *China-US University Presidents' Forum*, Chinese American Forum, 6/1/2005.

533: Verena Dobink, Associated Press, *13 Nations Denounced for Web Censorship*, chicagotribune.com/technology/, 11/7/2006.

534: Andrew Buncombe, Independent UK, *FCC Investigates Fake News*, alternet.org, 5/31/2006.

535: Fred Charatan, *Fake Prescription Drugs are Flooding the United States*, bmj.cig, 6/16/2001.

536: Chris Hanse, Dateline correspondent, *Traveling Through the World of Fake Drugs*, msnbc.msn.com/id/, 6/2/2006.

537: David Wallechninsky, *Is America Still Number 1?*, Parade, 1/14/2007.

541: Daljit Dhaliwal, Gene Sperling, Wideangle, *Back to School*, pbs.org/wnet/wideangle, 9/5/2006.

545: Rick Merritt, *For Academia, Patents Mean BIG $$*, Electronic Engineering Times, 4/24/2006.

546: Bob Keener, *Forbes 400 Richest Americans: They Didn't Do It Alone, Private Wealth Counts on Public Investment, Infrastructure*, ResponsibleWealth.org, 9/24/2004.

548: United States Government, *National Science Foundation History*, nsf.gov, 3/31/2006.

553: Michael D. Lemonick, *Are We Losing Our Edge?*, Time, 2/13/2006.

554: Anick Jesdanun, *AOL: Breach of Privacy Was a Mistake*, sfgate.com, 8/7/2006.

555: Tony Kontzer and Elisabeth Goodridge, *Privacy Group Alleges Monster-ous Breach*, informationweek.com, 9/10/2001.

561: Daniel W. Drezenr, Wideangle, *Offshore Outsourcing: Perceptions and Misperceptions*, pbs.org/wnet/wideangle, 9/13/2005.

562: *World BPO Forum Gateway to Business Process Outsourcing*, outsourcing.com, 12/13/2006.

564: Vinnee Tong, Associated Press, *Goldman CEO's $53.4M Bonus Breaks Record*, businessweek.com, 12/20/2006.

570: Robert E. Scott, Economic Policy Institute, *Increases in Foreign Liabilities Financed Through Sale of Government Securities*, epi.org, 6/30/2006.

576: Jordan Robertson, Associated Press, Miami Herald, *Engineer Indicted for Alleged Espionage*, herald.com, 12/14/2006.

577: Charles R. Smith, *China Is a Threat to America*, newsmax.com, 3/14/2002.

580: Foster Klug, Associated Press, *Congress Chides 4 Tech Giants Over China*, abcnews.go.com/Business, Web Date 15-Feb-06.

582: Associated Press, International Herald Tribune, *Police Arrest 10 Chinese Villagers in Dispute Over Paper Mill Pollution*, iht.com, 1/26/2007.

583: Joe McDonald, Associated Press, *China Expects $150B Trade Surplus*, washingtonpost.com, 11/10/2006.

584: Joe McDonald, Associated Press, *Date Set For China Bank's Record IPO*, thestar.com, 9/27/2006.

585: Excerpts from the Nudist on the Late Shift, *Could Anyone Have Thought up Hotmail?*, businessweek.com, Web Date 1-Nov-06.

590: CRN, *India's Tata Group Acquired Tyco Network At Bargain Price*, crn.com/sections/breakingnews, 11/1/2004.

591: Rajesh Mahapatra, Associated Press Writer, *IBM Develops New Technology to Help Improve Language Skills At India Call Centers*, post-gazete.com, 11/6/2006.

592: TiE website, *TiE Website*, tie.org, Web Date 17-Oct-06.

595: Gavin Rabinowitz, Associated Press, *Politics, Crime Go Hand-in-Hand in India*, bellsouth.net, 2006.

597: BusinessWeek Online, *The Future of Technology: The Big Trends Ahead and Our Ranking of the Top 100 Info Tech Companies*, businessweek.com, 2005.

598: Aaron Richadela, InformationWeek, *Invented in India*, informationweek.com, 2/13/2006.

608: Rohan Sullivan, Associated Press Writer, *Cheney Criticizes China's Arms Buildup*, guardian.co.uk/worldlatest/story, 2/23/2007.

609: Associated Press, International Institute for Strategic Studies, *Rumsfeld Questions China Military Buildup*, iiss.org, 6/3/2005.

615: Ron Schneiderman, Contributing Editor, *Offshoring. Outsourcing. Out of Work.*, Electronic Design, 10/20/2005.

616: Muzaffar Chishti, Migration Policy Institute, *Migration Information Source*, migrationimformation.org/Feature, 2/1/2007.

617: Sarala V. Nagala, Stanford Journal of International Relations, *India's Story of Success: Promoting the Information Technology Industry*, stanford.edu/group/sjir, 6/1/2005.

618: Wikipedia, *Non-Resident Indian and Person of Indian Origin*, en.wikipedia.org/wiki/Non-resident Indian and Person of Indian Origin, Web Date 9-Mar-07.

620: Richard Wallace, Mike Clendenin, and Sufia Tippu, *India the Last Frontier*, Electronic Engineering Times, 3/26/2007.

621: John Edwards, Contributing Editor, *Military R&D 101*, Electronic Design, 9/1/2006.

623: AFP, http://www.energybulleting.net, *China, India Fight for African Oil*, http://www.taipeitimes.com/News/worldbiz/archives/2004/10/16 , 10/15/2004.

624: Rule of law, *Clean Hands Doctrine*, Legal terminology.

629: Ganapati Mudur, New Delhi, *India to Introduce Death Penalty for Peddling Fake Drugs*, bmj.com, 8/23/2003.

630: Walt Bogdanich, Jake Hooker, New York Times, *Tainted Medicine -- a Secret Killer*, sfgate.com, 5/6/2007.

631: Terry J. Allen, *Counterfeit Drugs" Infected with Greed*, inthesetimes.com, 10/5/2006.

639: *About the Host: Fareed Zakaria*, foreignexchange.tv, Web Date 4-Nov-07.

640: Show 321 Transcript, *Sizing Up the Competition*, foreignexchange.tv, 5/25/2007.

641: Wikipedia, *Fareed Zakaria*, en.wikipedia.org/wiki/Fareed Zakaria, Web Date 4-Nov-07.

643: Website, *Asian-Silicon Valley Connection*, asvc.org/history.asp, Web Date 21-Sep-07.

645: Chi-Dooh Li, *In trade, China's Moral Compass is Off Course*, seattlepi.nwscource.com, 9/14/2007.

650: Brian Williams, Mara Schiavocampo, *Globalization Gets Personal*, MSNBC Nightly News, 1/16/2008.

652: *The TiE That Binds Could Bring in $800 M By 2006*, financialexpress.com, 1/6/2003.

654: Audra Ang, The Associated Press, *China Drug Official Given Death Sentence*, abcnews.go.com, Web Date 6-Jul-07.

655: *Counterfeit drugs: A Rising Public Health Problem*, webmd.com, 10/18/2004.

658: Heather Timmons and Somini Sengupta, *Building a Modern Arsenal in India*, nytimes.com/2007, 8/31/2007.

669: Associated Press, Washington, *Defense Department Analyst, Former Boeing Employee, 2 Chinese Immigrants, Arrested in 2 Spy Cases*, foxnews.com, 2/11/2008.

671: Christian E. Weller, Holly Wheeler, *Our Nation's Surprising Technology Trade Deficit*, americanprogress.org/issues, 3/10/2008.

673: Richard Wallace, *India Rides Growth Wave Into New Age of Tech Globalization*, Electronic Engineering Times, 2/25/2008.

681: Knowledg@Wharton, *Indian Companies Are on an Acquisition Spree: Their Target" U.S. Firms*, knowledge.wharton.upenn.edu, 12/13/2006.

683: *21 and the World is Yours*, ABC News, 4/7/2008.

684: Sachar Bar-On, *China Investment An Open Book?*, cbsnews.com, 4/6/2008, Web Date 7-Apr-08.

685: Francis C. Assisi, *Skilled Indian Immigrants Create Wealth for America*, indolink.com, 1/4/2007.

691: Bruce Japsen and David Greising, *Baxter CEO Tells Congress Heparin Tampering was Deliberate*, chicagotribune.com/business/, 4/29/2008.

707: Patrick Mannion, *Dubai's Silicon Dawn -- Dubai" From Sand to Silicon*, eeTimes, 5/26/2008.

712: Edward Iwata, *U.S. Considers Costly Switch to International Accounting Rules*, usatoday.com, Web Date 1-Jan-09.

715: *Awash in Counterfeit Drugs, India May Pay More for Foreign Approval*, blogs.wsj.com/health, 5/14/2008.

718: An Endangered American Professional, *A California Reader Draws The Connection Between Heavy H-1B Usage and Corporate Fraud, Big Financial Losses*, vdare.com, Web Date 11-Dec-08.

721: Manjeet Kripalani in Bombay, *Private Equity Pours Into India*, businessweek.com, 6/20/2005.

722: Richard Behar, *World Bank's Web of Ties to 'India's Enron'*, foxnews.com, 1/12/2009.

738: Capital Eye Communications, *TARP Recipients Paid Out $114 Million for Politicking Last Year*, opensecrets.org, 2/4/2009.

769: Kofi Annan, Cnet, *Kofi Annan's IT Challenge to Silicon Valley*, umsl.edu, 11/5/2002.

772: Jennifer Bjorhus, SiliconValley.com, *Slowdown Sending Tech Jobs Overseas*, umsl.edu, 10/21/2002.

775: Reuters, New York Times, *Intel to Invest Up to $200 Million in India*, umsl.edu, 8/30/2002.

777: Indian Express, *China's Software Exports Only Four Years Behind India: Gartner*, umsl.edu, 9/23/2002.

879: Joshua Rhett Miller, *Internet Traffic from U.S. government Websites Was Redirected via Chinese Servers*, foxnews.com, 11/16/2010.

887: IANS, *Indias Holding Dual Citizenship Must have Tax Obligations in India*, thaindian.com, 1/8/2010.

901: Pauline Jelink, The Associated Press, *Report: Too Many Whites, Men Leading Military*, navytimes.com, 3/7/2011.

921: Tony Munroe and Peter Henderson, *India's IT Aims to Soften Image as Obama Visits*, reuters.com, 10/27/2010.

923: Ted C. Fishman, *Why the Jobs are Going Over There*, usatoday.com, 5/17/2011.

926: BBC News South Asia, *Corruption 'Threatens India's Economic Growth'*, bbc.co.uk/news/worl-south-asia, 3/15/2011.

928: Brett Arends, MarketWatch, *IMF Bobshell: Age of America Nears End*, marketwatch.com, 4/25/2011.

929: Patrick Thibodeau, ComputerWorld, *Greenspan: H-1B Cap Would Make U.S. Workers 'Privileged Elite'*, computerworld.com, 4/30/2009.

930: Kurt Nimmo, *Greenspan: Dumb Americans Deserve Unemployment*, infowars.com, 7/15/2011.

945: Barbara Micale, *Mergers, Economic Espionage, China, Called Key IT Issues*, Pamplin College of Business, VirginiaTech, 2006.

947: Associated Press, *FDA Blocks Generic Drug Imports from India*, usatoday.com, 9/16/2008.

948: Alan R. Spies, Virgil Van Dusen, *Counterfeit Drugs A Menace Keeps Growing*, US Pharmacist, 1/15/2003.

950: Alan Silverleib, *U.S. Power, Influence Will Decline in Future Report Says*, cnn.com, 11/21/2008.

951: Roxana Tiron, *Joint Chiefs Chairman Reiterates Security Threat of High Debt*, thehill.com, 6/24/2010.

952: Associated Press, *FBI Warns Brewing Cyberwar May Have Same Impact as 'Well-Placed Bomb'*, foxnews.com, 3/8/2010.

953: Associated Press, *U.S. Engineer Convicted of Selling Secrets to China*, usatoday.com, 8/9/2010.

954: Associated Press, *Pentagon Discloses Largest-Ever Cyber Theft*, foxnews.com, 7/14/2011.

956: Jay Bavisi and Joseph M. Grim, *Biggest National Security Threat: Cyber Attack*, foxbusiness.com, 7/26/2010.

957: Associated Press, *Pentagon Cyber Commamnd to Create Force for Digital Warfare*, foxnews.com, 5/5/2009.

958: John Blackstone, *Google Not Only Target of China Hackers*, cbsnews.com, 1/24/2010.

959: Patrick J. Buchanan, *Who Fed the Tiger?*, wnd.com, 11/18/2010.

960: Associated Press, *Chinese Spy Meng Sentenced to 24 Months*, jonathanpollard.org, 6/18/2008.

961: Associated Press, *How a Networking Immigrant Became a Chinese Spy*, cbsnews.com, 5/9/2011.

962: Bill Gertz, *Cyber-attack on U.S. Firms, Google Traced To Chinese*, washingtontimes.com, 3/24/2010.

963: Sudeep Reddy, *White House Aims to Lure More Foreign Investment*, wsj.com, 10/10/2011.

965: NSF, *Award Summary: By State/Institution FY2010*, bfa.nsf.gov/AwdLst2, Web Date 29-Oct-11.

983: *Chinese Applicants to U.S. Schools Skyrocket.*, patriotupdate.com, 1/12/2012.

986: Wall Street Journal, *Pentagon Sounds Alarm at China's Military Buildup*, foxnews.com, 8/17/2010.

987: Alec Liu, *U.S. Could Lose the SciTech Edge to China, Experts Fear*, foxnews.com, 11/1/2010.

988: Fox News, *NIH Funds $2.6 Million Study to Get Prostitutes in China to Drink Less*, foxnews.com, 5/14/2009.

989: Bill Gertz, *Senators Want China to Assist Probe of Counterfeit Weapons Parts*, washingtontimes.com, 6/14/2011.

990: Battelle, *2011 Global R&D Forecast*, rdmag.com, 12/1/2010.

994: Center for Immigration Studies, *Three Decades of Mass Immigration: The Legacy of the 1965 Immigration Act*, cis.org/articles/1995, 9/1/1995.

997: Hudson Institute, *Index of Global Philantropy and Remittances 2011*, 1015 15th Street, NW, Washington DC, 2011.

998: *The Financial Times: Corruption Besets India*, businessday.co.za, 3/26/2012.

999: *Retiring FBI Official Says Current Cybersecurity Strategy 'Unsustainable'*, foxnews.com, 3/27/2012.

1001: Daniel Golden, *American Universities Infected by foreign Spies Detected by FBI*, bloomberg.com, 4/8/2012.

1002: Hari Kumar, *Why Has India Become the world's Top Arms Buyer?*, The New York Times India Ink, 3/21/2012.

1003: Fox News, *US Government Spent at Least $945M on Advertising in 2010*, foxnews.com, 3/19/2012.

1004: Josh Benstein and Shalini Sharma, *License to Terrorize*, thedaily.com, 4/2/2012.

1005: Virginia Tech Pamplin College of Business Magazine, *Education Needs In Iraq*, Spring 2010.

1006: Rep Tim Huelskamp, *Obamacare HHS Rule Would Give Government Everybody's Health Records*, washingtonexaminer.com, 9/23/2011.

1009: Colin Barr, *How Foreigners Will Buy the U.S.*, finance.fortune.cnn.com, 5/18/2011.

1010: Sabrina Tavernise, *Whites Account for Under Half of Births in US*, nytimes.com, 5/17/2012.

1011: Emily Esfahani Smith, *Fareed Zakaria Digs into Glenn Beck, Says Birtherism is 'coded' Race-Talk*, theblaze.com, 4/1/2011.

1012: Fox News, *Bomb Suspect's Citizenship Raises Questions About Naturalization Process*, foxnews.com, 5/4/10 .

1013: John Byrne, *Kagan Helped Shield Saudis for 9/11 Lawsuits*, rawstory.com, 5/11/2010.

1014: Karl Huus, *Islamic Schools on Rise in US, Look for Acceptance*, msnbc.msn.com, 6/13/2011.

1032: Terence P. Jeffery, *Obama Increased Foreign Aid 80%; Spent 76% More on Foreign Aid Than Border Security*, cnsnews.com, 10/2/2012.

1035: The World Bank, *Migration and Remittances Factbook 2011 2nd Edition*, , 1/1/2011.

1042: Christopher S. Rugaber, AP Economics Writer, *Foreign Holdings of US Debt Hit Record $5.48T*, ap.org, 12/17/2012.

1063: Craig Timberg and Amy Gardner, *Democrats Push to Redeploy Obama's Voter Database*, washingtonpost.com, 11/20/2012.

1064: *Chocolate Cake, Please: How an Engineer Became a Scholar of Consumer Behavior*, Pamplin College of Business: Putting IT to Work, Fall 2012.

1065: Ben Shapiro, *Permanent Campaign: Obama to Use Re-Election Machine to Target NRA*, breitbart.com, 1/17/2013.

Index

How to Take Back Our Jobs and Build a Bright Future.

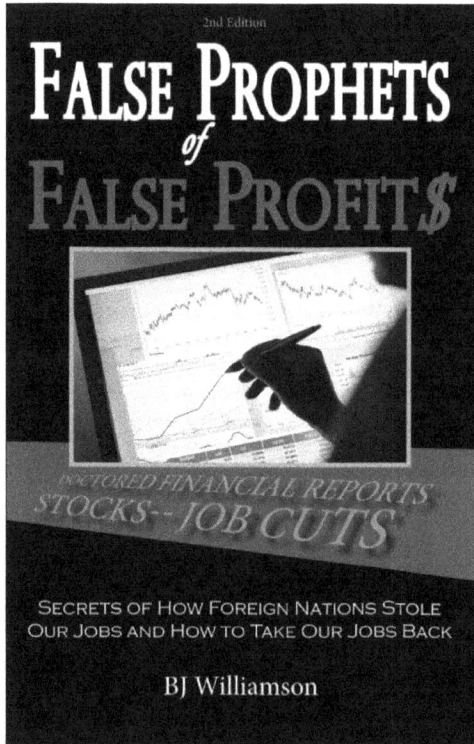

Learn the hidden secrets behind job losses to foreign workers, and how foreign investments manipulated our stock market. You will find many surprises, and most importantly an economic model that shows how we can restore our economic prosperity.

To Order False Prophets of False Profits

go to: *Amazon.com*

Or to learn more go to: *www.lanitepublishing.com*

How Foreign Nations are Using Our Own
Political System Against US

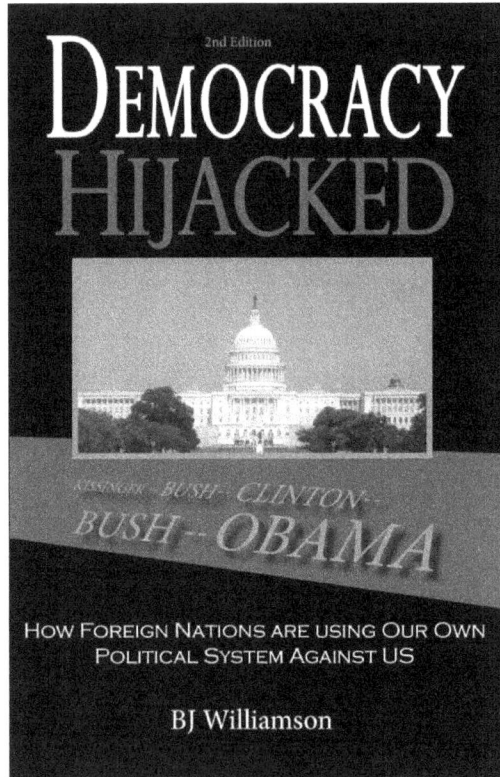

Discover how foreign nations are using outsourcing money to manipulate our elections, and how corporate executives are recruited to become lobbyists to get legislation passed that enables transferring our jobs to foreign workers using visas and offshoring.

To Order Democracy Hijacked

go to: *Amazon.com*

Or to learn more go to: *www.lanitepublishing.com*

www.ingramcontent.com/pod-product-compliance
Lightning Source LLC
Chambersburg PA
CBHW060555200326
41521CB00007B/577